ICOR® JOURNEY

Learn how to build your ultimate productivity system with any tools!

Tom Solid and Paco Cantero

Paperless Movement®

Dedicated to our loved ones and to all the busy professionals who grapple daily with stress, anxiety, and overwhelm from the constant flood of information and action.

CONTENTS

Productivity System

Beast

3, 2, 1... IGNITION!

BEHIND THE INK: THE DRIVING FORCE THAT SHAPED THIS BOOK

"The big secret in life is that there is no big secret. Whatever your goal, you can get there if you're willing to work." — Oprah Winfrey

Since the inception of Paperless Movement® in 2018, we've had the privilege of connecting with hundreds of thousands of busy professionals caught in the relentless whirl of information and action overload.

These individuals, much like yourself, navigated through the fog of stress, anxiety, and the heavy burden of unmet goals. Their stories were ones of time, energy, money, and resources slipping through their fingers; missed deadlines and unmanaged teams becoming all too common in their narratives.

In response, we introduced them to ICOR®, a transformative methodology and approach that reshaped their approach to the world of productivity.

This wasn't just about getting more done in less time; it was about redefining their relationship with tools, work, and success.

Through the comprehensive concepts and workflows we provided, they crafted personalized productivity systems with the perfect tool stack. These systems weren't just effective; they were sustainable, liberating them from the cycle of burnout, tool switching, and underachievement.

With the support of the Paperless Movement® Membership, the structured path of the ICOR® Journey, and the close-knit community of our INNER CIRCLE Program, success stories multiplied.

Yet, through the invaluable feedback of our community, we realized a gap in our offering.

What was missing?

A gateway; an accessible entry point to the core principles of ICOR® and a touchstone for deepening understanding and application of our decades-tested methodology.

This book is that missing piece.

It's a distillation of our insights and experiences, designed to be your companion in navigating the complexities of productivity and personal achievement.

We know we can't cover all the services and products we offer, like the Paperless Movement® Membership and our INNER CIRCLE Program, in a static piece of content like this book.

Why?

Because, at the Paperless Movement® Membership, you can dive much deeper into the ICOR® Journey with video lessons, Magic Slides that summarize key concepts and workflows for better understanding, and implementation videos showing how these concepts and workflows are literally applied across various software tools. There are also many additional services you can check on the Paperless Movement® website.

Our top-tier service is the INNER CIRCLE Program, where you get direct access to Tom and Paco, the founders of the Paperless Movement® and authors of this book. Through coaching live sessions, participants can seek guidance and address their unique needs, ensuring they can effectively implement the insights gained.

As productivity is an ongoing and endless journey, a book alone can't achieve complete productivity. That's why we offer these additional services, to guarantee we cover all your needs.

However, by reading this book, we guarantee you'll achieve these five main goals:

1. Experience productivity from a radically different, life-

changing perspective.

2. Gain a clear understanding of what a productivity system is.
3. Get a powerful introduction to ICOR®'s principles and start incorporating them effortlessly.
4. Build a solid foundational core to design and develop your own productivity system.
5. Have a quick-reference guide at your fingertips to revisit any concept or workflow without wasting time, providing instant clarity on any aspect of your productivity system based on ICOR®.

We've poured our hearts into these pages, and we hope you find within them the inspiration and guidance we've aimed to provide.

Thank you for giving us your most valuable asset: your time. We deeply appreciate it!

Welcome to a new chapter of your productivity journey. We're thrilled to embark on it with you because this is the journey you've always been searching for.

Welcome to the ICOR® Journey!

A PERSONAL INVITATION: ARE YOU THE READER WE'VE BEEN WAITING FOR?

"You never change things by fighting the existing reality. To change something, build a new model that makes the existing model obsolete." — Buckminster Fuller

This book, like all our creations, is crafted with a specific audience in mind: YOU, the busy professional. Now, you might be pondering: What exactly defines a busy professional?

In our eyes, this encompasses a broad spectrum of individuals: CEOs, C-level executives, business owners, freelancers, entrepreneurs, solopreneurs, project managers, team members, directors, department heads...

Essentially, anyone immersed in the corporate sphere who faces the daily challenge of sifting through a mountain of information, eager to transform it into clear, actionable steps toward achieving their goals.

Let's face it; information, in the absence of action, is both meaningless and a missed opportunity.

It's crucial to recognize we've transcended the so-called Information Era. What we're navigating now is far more complex and demanding: it's the Information Management Era.

In the bustling landscape of today's knowledge economy, true wealth is born from your prowess in staying one step ahead, out-thinking and out-learning those around you.

Mastering the art of information and action management is no longer just an asset; it's the cornerstone skill, the key that unlocks success and sets you apart from the competition.

The winners of this era are those who excel at transforming information into strategic decisions and taking action on them. The rest are left behind, struggling to keep pace.

Through the pages of this book, we invite you to embark on a transformative journey toward mastering the art of information and action management.

We're not just talking about getting by in today's fast-paced world. We're talking about excelling, leading the way, and turning your aspirations into reality.

It's about more than surviving. It's about thriving by creating, planning, executing, and completing actions that catapult you toward your goals.

Welcome to your path to success.

FROM OUR WORLD TO YOURS: INTRODUCING OURSELVES

"Working hard for something we don't care about is called stress; working hard for something we love is called passion." — *Simon Sinek*

B efore we dive into the transformative world of ICOR®, you're likely eager to learn about the "visionaries" behind this groundbreaking methodology.

What fuels their drive? And why do they believe so strongly that ICOR® will redefine your productivity landscape?

Let's meet Tom Solid and Paco Cantero, the trailblazers at the helm of this revolution.

Dr. Thomas Roedl, better known as Tom Solid, is more than just a figurehead.

His odyssey commenced in the demanding arena of corporate efficiency, where he achieved the remarkable feat of boosting team productivity by an astonishing 60%, all without increasing the headcount.

This achievement not only garnered him widespread recognition but also propelled him into a pivotal role as a Business Analyst, where he led initiatives to streamline operations across two IT teams.

His crowning achievement came when he successfully implemented Asana for over a thousand global employees at F. Hoffmann-La Roche, markedly enhancing productivity and production processes.

In 2018, Tom's desire to uplift professionals worldwide led him to establish the Paperless Movement®, with Paco Cantero joining as a co-founder in the journey four years later.

Paco Cantero, hooked on technology and process optimization, began coding at the tender age of eight.

During his computer science engineering studies, he gained

invaluable experience working with five multinational corporations, eventually joining industry behemoths like PriceWaterhouseCoopers and Accenture. There, he was instrumental in refining and optimizing corporate processes and technologies.

Paco's seamless transition from a sought-after consultant to the successful management of four businesses and a team of over 70 individuals, without the aid of a personal assistant, is nothing less than extraordinary.

Having launched his first enterprise in 2002, Paco's evolution is a testament to the efficacy of ICOR®, highlighting his exceptional skills in fostering efficiency and organization.

His journey not only shows the power of our methodology but also serves as a beacon, illustrating the heights of productivity and control that busy professionals can achieve.

Together, Tom and Paco embody the essence of ICOR®.

Their dedication is not just about advocating a methodology; it's about living it, proving that with the right concepts, workflows, tools, and guidance, unlocking your full potential is not just possible: it's unavoidable.

THE PAPERLESS MOVEMENT® DECODED: A MANIFESTO FOR THE DIGITAL AGE

"To improve is to change; to be perfect is to change often." — *Winston Churchill*

The Paperless Movement® began as a mission to transition busy professionals from the tangible clutter of paper to the sleek efficiency of digital information.

This goal, though ambitious, soon revealed itself as merely a small spark that ignited a massive blaze.

The real question emerged: Now that everything is digitized, how do I harness its full potential?

This "curiosity" was the catalyst for the creation of ICOR®, a methodology where information meets action.

When Paco Cantero joined The Movement, we recognized the need to weave a tapestry of clear, unwavering values into the very soul of our mission. After all, a project without values is like a ship without a rudder: directionless and doomed to fail.

It was through this realization that we defined our core values, principles designed to maximize your value gain.

Here they are, presented for you:

- **No fluff**. We deliver only the most essential content. In a pragmatic world, our approach is straightforward: Learn today, apply immediately.
- **Focus**. We understand that attention is a scarce commodity for the busy professional. Our strategies are designed to enhance focus and peak performance without the burnout.
- **Time-obsessed**. Your time is precious, and we vow never to waste it. Our respect for your schedule is paramount, and we're here to show you how to make every second count.
- **Simplicity**. Our years of productivity experience

have been distilled into easily digestible concepts and workflows you can implement instantly. We've done the heavy lifting so you can enjoy the fruits of simplicity.

- **Cool productivity**. We believe productivity shouldn't be a drag. Life is meant for joy, laughter, and enjoyment, and we're here to prove that productivity can be just as cool.
- **Processes first**. Our philosophy places concepts and processes above tools. With a focus on workflows, we equip you to navigate tools flexibly, ensuring your productivity is never handcuffed to a single solution.
- **Long-term believers**. Our commitment is to enduring solutions, not fleeting hacks. We share strategies that have stood the test of time, promising practices that will continue to serve you well into the future, regardless of technological advances.
- **All about busy professionals**. We deeply understand the challenges busy professionals face: overwhelm, anxiety, and the constant battle with priorities. We've been in your shoes, and we know how to remove those negative feelings.

LAYERED LEARNING: HOW THIS BOOK UNFOLDS

"Order and simplification are the first steps toward mastery of a subject." — Thomas Mann

At the Paperless Movement®, we're all about keeping things digestible, straightforward, and right to the point. This book embodies that ethos, making understanding its structure a breeze.

In the first section, we kick things off by breaking down three pivotal concepts that are essential to grasp.

These ideas are not just foundational; they're recurring themes that will weave through our narrative.

Grasping these concepts is your first step towards a transformative perspective on productivity. They will guide your intuition, helping you navigate the vast world of information and action, and more importantly, the selection of tools that will maximize your effectiveness in building the productivity system of your dreams.

With the groundwork laid, we'll dive into the heart of this book: the ICOR® Journey. This is the best and fastest way to implement ICOR®.

This second section is a practical, step-by-step journey to move from information to actionable outcomes that will not just meet but exceed your goals.

Each stage of ICOR® (Input, Control, Output, Refine) is meticulously detailed, distinguishing between essential concepts and pragmatic workflows.

ICOR® is designed to be flexible with the tools you use (in fact, they don't matter at all), which is why understanding its core concepts and workflows is so important.

Here's why this flexibility is a game-changer.

Because ICOR® is adaptable to any tool, you're free to choose from the entire range of options out there. This flexibility lets you work with tools you're already familiar with or those your company has in place, even if they wouldn't be your top pick.

However, being tool-independent doesn't mean ICOR® leaves you in the dark about choosing the right tools. In fact, guiding you to the best tools is one of the areas where ICOR® really shines.

We're committed to helping you find the perfect set of tools that ensures peak performance without the risk of burnout.

The ultimate aim of ICOR® is to assist you in creating and fine-tuning your productivity system end to end, equipped with the tools that best suit your needs.

In the third section of the book, we encapsulate our closing thoughts on ICOR® and next steps for you, offering guidance on how to best embrace and leverage the methodology for maximum benefit, thanks to additional products and services we've carefully crafted to move your productivity, literally, to the next level.

The book concludes with an appendix, serving as a quick-reference glossary for any ICOR® terminology introduced. This resource is designed to save you time, providing clear definitions at your fingertips, whether you're midway through the book or applying its principles in real life.

Consider it your go-to reference, accessible at any stage of your reading or application process, ensuring clarity and ease as you navigate through the concepts and workflows.

We've tailored this book with you, the busy professional, in mind.

This chapter is more than an introduction; it's an invitation to join us on a journey towards unparalleled productivity and well-being, grounded in values that drive success and fulfillment.

Welcome to a journey that understands you, champions your growth, and supports you from the very first page.

SECTION 1 - ICOR®
CORE CONCEPTS

1.1 BEYOND TOOLS: CONCEPTS AS YOUR PRODUCTIVITY COMPASS

"It's not about ideas. It's about making ideas happen." —
Steve Jobs

B efore we delve into the three pivotal concepts that will reshape your approach to ICOR®, let's pause for a moment to consider why grasping these concepts is so crucial.

For the busy professional, every minute is a treasure, and understanding the core principles that drive your actions transforms from a mere preference to an absolute need.

The ICOR® Journey is not about accumulating knowledge for its own sake but about refining your life to maximize every moment and the way you work.

Concepts stand as beacons of understanding, illuminating the path to saving time, optimizing resources, and elevating your productivity to heights you haven't even imagined.

The realm of theory, with its intricate labyrinths of abstraction, is one we navigate with caution. Like you, we focus on the real-world impact of theoretical knowledge, boiling it down to its most potent representation: concepts.

Picture yourself trying to find your way through a dense forest without a compass. That's what navigating the professional world feels like without a solid grasp of concepts. They serve as your guide, giving your actions purpose and direction. Without this guidance, you're simply going through the motions, disconnected from the meaning behind your actions.

In the world of productivity, the relentless search for the "perfect tool" often ends in disappointment. That's because the key to a truly effective productivity system doesn't lie in the tools themselves but in understanding the underlying concepts and workflows that inform their use.

This book aims to distill every piece of advice to its essence, ensuring that the insights we share are both actionable and impactful.

Investing in the understanding of concepts is akin to laying the foundation of a ship. It's what gives your productivity system direction and resilience. Far from being just academic jargon, concepts are the building blocks of practical productivity.

Taking the time to master these concepts is an investment in your future efficiency, enabling you not only to use tools and workflows but to adapt and innovate them to fit your unique needs.

1.2 ICOR® UNVEILED: CRAFTING PEAK PRODUCTIVITY IN A FAST-PACED WORLD

"Productivity is being able to do things that you were never able to do before." — Franz Kafka

I n our whirlwind of a world, the pursuit of peak efficiency and productivity isn't just a goal; it's a necessity.

At the core of ICOR® lies a holistic philosophy and methodology, meticulously crafted to enhance every aspect of both professional and personal lives. This approach ensures that information, tasks, projects, and team communications are handled with unmatched efficiency, propelling productivity to new heights.

ICOR® isn't merely a set of procedures; it's a comprehensive methodology designed to elevate productivity beyond the simple act of finishing tasks or absorbing information.

ICOR® champions a harmonious, integrated strategy that not only aligns with your professional ambitions and lifestyle but also sets a definitive aim: to empower busy professionals to craft, establish, and maintain a seamless productivity system, equipped with a perfectly tailored suite of tools.

As we delve deeper, the ICOR® Journey lays out a roadmap not just for attaining efficiency but for nurturing a rewarding and orderly approach to your work life thanks to ICOR®. This methodology untangles the complexities of a productivity system end to end.

It goes beyond the mere selection and implementation of optimal tools; it's about converting information into actionable steps towards your goals, guided by intuition, minimizing energy waste, and achieving peak performance without the risk of burnout.

ICOR® guides you from information acquisition to action, delineated by its four pivotal stages:

1. **Input**. Gathering essential information from the external environment into your domain, or drawing directly from your innermost thoughts and reflections.
2. **Control**. Processing this raw data into actionable tasks, charting the course for what comes next.
3. **Output**. Implementing these tasks to generate tangible results, outcomes that mark the progression towards your goals, no matter if they're generated by you or your team.
4. **Refine**. Enhancing your productivity system with the principles of iteration and refinement, surpassing simple software solutions.

These stages form the backbone of your bespoke productivity system end to end, a topic we will deeply explore throughout this book.

1.3 THE KEYSTONE OF DIGITAL PRODUCTIVITY: SINGLE SOURCE OF TRUTH (SSOT)

"A place for everything, and everything in its place." —
Samuel Smiles

In our lightning-fast digital era, managing our ever-growing digital footprint has become a monumental task.

That's where the concept of a Single Source of Truth (SSOT) shines as a guiding light, helping you navigate through the clutter of our digital world.

SSOT goes beyond mere storage solutions; it's the definitive reference point for both action and information storage and retrieval.

Here we share a few examples to better understand the wide scope of SSOT and see how powerful it becomes to make all the difference:

- **Conversation threads**. Tools like Slack use threads to house all relevant responses, making them the SSOT for that conversation or topic.
- **Custom views in software**. A custom view in your Project Management system displaying your team's Weekly Goals can be your SSOT for them, showing only a specific part of the system's content you need.
- **Documents**. Corporate SOPs (Standard Operating Procedures) serve as the SSOT, detailing every step of a process to eliminate confusion.
- **Tasks**. A task in your Task Management system, packed with all the necessary info, acts as the SSOT for that task.

SSOT embodies the clarity and simplicity we all crave, guiding us to precisely where each piece of information or action belongs and how to swiftly locate it when needed.

This concept empowers you to build the productivity system

of your dreams; one that's coherent, efficient, and leverages the best tools available.

Imagine the liberation of designing a system tailored precisely to your needs, without any constraints.

SSOT affords you the flexibility to combine different tools, capitalizing on their strengths and sidestepping their weaknesses (because no tool is perfect).

For instance, in Project Management, this means you're free to use multiple tools for different aspects of your work, choosing the best features from each. By clearly defining the purpose and use of each tool, you remove any confusion about where things belong or where to find them, ensuring your productivity system operates like a well-oiled machine.

You can also consider, for example, the possibility of creating a robust Task Management system using a mix of tools like Superhuman, Slack, Todoist, and ClickUp.

You can tap into the Task Management capabilities of these tools to handle multiple kinds of tasks: Superhuman for tasks that come from emails, Slack for tasks stemming from chat threads or conversations, Todoist for your personal tasks, and ClickUp for coordinating tasks with your team.

While it might seem daunting at first, defining the specific use of each tool eradicates any potential for confusion. You'll always know where to store and retrieve information or actions, streamlining your workflow and reducing stress. And in the end, that's the hallmark of an effective productivity system.

At its core, SSOT is about how you use your tools, not the tools themselves.

It's a strategy for intelligently organizing your information and tasks in a way that resonates with you. By judiciously selecting and integrating tools, you can devise a customized productivity system that perfectly aligns with your requirements.

SSOT transcends the simple approach of consolidating your data into a single location. It's about clever organization, effortless access, and harnessing the strengths of multiple tools to enhance your workflow.

By thoughtfully pairing tools that complement each other, you can create a digital ecosystem that amplifies your work style, enabling you to achieve more with minimal fuss.

That's the true essence and power of a SSOT.

1.4 UNVEILING THE ICOR® FRAMEWORK: THE STORY BEHIND A GATEWAY TO A NEW DAWN IN PRODUCTIVITY

"We shape our tools, and thereafter our tools shape us."
— Marshall McLuhan

In the heart of every busy professional pulses a unified dream: to devise a productivity system that not only steers us toward our goals with efficiency and effectiveness but does so by harnessing the best tools without the drain of our valuable time, energy, or money.

Our fascination with these tools springs from their potential to unlock our fullest productivity.

Yet, the pursuit of the ideal tool stack often leads us into a quagmire of choices, leaving us more enervated than empowered. We've navigated these choppy waters, spending endless hours on tools that promised much but delivered little. Well, we bet you're already familiar with the story...

This collective quandary propelled us, at the Paperless Movement®, to pool every ounce of our energy and resources into crafting a real solution. And we're thrilled to announce: We've cracked the code!

Introducing the ICOR® Framework, a groundbreaking approach that offers you a blueprint for a cohesive, streamlined productivity system end to end.

This isn't just any solution. It's one meticulously tailored to your needs, ensuring optimal use of a minimal set of tools for maximum efficiency.

Though it may sound almost too good to be true, we assure you, this is a reality we're excited to unfold for you. Let us share with you the genesis of our quest.

Our mission was crystal clear from the get-go: to empower you to effortlessly curate your ideal set of tools, paving your way to what we like to call "productivity nirvana."

The ultimate goal?

A seamless melding of tools that works in perfect harmony, allowing you to glide through information and action with the focus squarely on results, success, and growth.

This journey, while ambitious, started as a mere dream; a flicker of possibility that, as history has shown, is how all transformative solutions begin.

Our search for the perfect productivity blueprint spanned not just months but years and decades. This dedication wasn't about boasting but about resolving a significant challenge that could transform your efficiency in a matter of hours. Yes: hours!

We've distilled our journey into a straightforward, actionable tool you can apply right now. This isn't about adding another tool to your arsenal. It's about giving you a comprehensive overview of your productivity system, enabling you to craft a workflow that's a mirror image of your thought process.

Our breakthrough realization was the interconnectedness and overlapping nature of our digital and professional spheres. They're not distinct paths but intertwined trails.

This "overlapping moment" is critical. It addresses the common struggle of creating a seamless productivity system and choosing the right tools without redundancy or gaps. Here's how it goes.

The ICOR® Framework splits into four key areas: Personal and Business, plus Information and Action.

Think of Personal as your solo work zone, where it's just you, different from Business, where teamwork and collaboration come into play.

On the other side, Information deals with knowledge

management, while Action is all about getting things done.

What's cool about the ICOR® Framework is how it visually lays out these four areas, using different colors, so you can easily see how they overlap and connect.

This is super important because it helps you see the big picture of how everything fits together, which is crucial when you're trying to build a seamless productivity system and choose the right tools without doubling up or missing a beat.

It's all about spotting where things overlap. This helps you avoid the trap of picking tools that don't really serve your system well, which can lead to confusion, inefficiency, or just feeling stuck.

With the ICOR® Framework, you place each tool within these areas to see exactly what it's meant for, compare it with others like it, find any overlaps (where you might be using two tools when one would do), spot any missing pieces, and weed out any tools that don't add value.

The ICOR® Framework also helps you understand three crucial concepts: Core Apps, Satellite Apps, and Utility Apps.

Core Apps are essential. They offer a wide range of features and serve as the primary repository for your information and action (your Single Source of Truth).

You can't remove these apps without a replacement because they hold crucial data and functionalities.

Switching from one Core App to another is often painful, expensive, and risky. Even if your current Core App has some issues, switching usually brings its own set of challenges. It's often better to stick with your existing Core App despite any frustrations.

Satellite Apps, on the other hand, enhance your Core Apps.

They help reduce friction or address weaknesses in your Core Apps for specific tasks like capturing, automating workflows, or linking different systems.

Unlike Core Apps, you can easily swap Satellite Apps when you find a better one, as the impact on your overall productivity system is minimal. For example, Superhuman is a Satellite App that enhances email management tools like Google Mail or Outlook, allowing you to manage emails faster without changing your core email system.

Understanding the difference between Core and Satellite Apps can help you make smarter choices about your software tools, leading to a more efficient and flexible decision-making process when considering whether to switch tools.

Finally, we have Utility Apps.

These are tools that boost your productivity but aren't essential, so your system won't fall apart if you stop using them. A couple of clear examples of these are internet browsers like Arc or launchers like Raycast.

As you can see, by using and interacting with the ICOR® Framework, you're crafting a productivity system that's perfectly suited to you. You gain the power to:

- Conduct a thorough analysis of each tool's role, ensuring it aligns with your needs.
- Directly compare tools within the same category, spotlighting their strengths and weaknesses.
- Identify redundancies and gaps, steering you towards a more efficient tool stack.
- Recognize and eliminate unnecessary tools, thereby decluttering your system.

By adopting the ICOR® Framework, you not only embark on crafting a system that's inherently yours but also join

The Paperless Movement® community, speaking a universal language of productivity. This collective wisdom saves time and boosts efficiency.

We encourage you to explore the ICOR® Framework by placing your current tools within it. If you need extra guidance, check out the Paperless Movement® website, where you'll find a video showing how to bring this concept to life.

After engaging with this book, revisit and refine your ICOR® Framework. The transformation you'll witness promises to be enlightening.

The ICOR® Framework is a paradigm shift designed by and for busy professionals. It's not merely a tool but your passport to a custom-built productivity system, the very system you've dreamt of, the one you richly deserve.

Welcome to the dawn of your new productive life.

SECTION 2 - THE ICOR® JOURNEY: THE COMPREHENSIVE STEP-BY-STEP GUIDE TO MASTERING ICOR® AND TURN INFORMATION INTO ACTION

"Complexity is your enemy. Any fool can make something complicated. It is hard to keep things simple."
— Richard Branson

Picture this: you're a busy professional buried under multiple projects, swamped with emails, and racing against deadlines.

Sound familiar?

We're pretty sure that might very well be your current reality, and that's why you're here.

With ICOR®, you start to efficiently sort through your information (Input), organize it effectively (Control), focus on impactful actions (Output), and constantly enhance the process (Refine).

This paragraph above highlights the transformative potential of ICOR®, showing how it's not just about excelling professionally but also about finding personal fulfillment and achieving a harmonious life balance.

Now, we reach the part you've been eagerly anticipating: the "how."

You've likely found resonance in what we've discussed so far, yet you're pondering: This sounds fantastic, but how do I actually apply this? How do I make it all come together?

Fear not, we're here to guide you.

This section is devoted entirely to walking you through the ICOR® Journey, stage by stage, step by step.

You'll grasp the parallels between these stages and the ICOR® Framework, mastering the essential concepts and workflows needed to craft the productivity system of your dreams.

This transformation is within reach because you'll establish a strong foundation that empowers you to progressively leverage every aspect, day after day, without falter.

Our method? The "layer approach."

We adhere to this strategy because it's the most direct and impactful way to offer tangible solutions to you; cutting through the noise and saving you time, a benefit that only grows with time.

This approach has already transformed the work lives of countless professionals via the ICOR® Journey, a meticulously designed program encompassing five in-depth courses accessible through our Paperless Movement® Membership.

Each course is structured around three foundational layers: concepts, workflows, and implementation.

In this book, we primarily explore the concepts and workflows layers, as the hands-on nature of implementation, especially with specific software tools, extends beyond what we can cover in written form.

Nevertheless, rest assured, we've integrated numerous practical examples throughout the book. These examples are designed to seamlessly connect theoretical insights with real-world applications, providing you with a solid foundation to effectively implement these strategies on your own.

This ensures you're well-prepared to craft and refine your productivity system, even beyond the pages of this book.

Ready to jump in?

LET'S ICOR®!

2. 1 STAGE 1: INPUT (INFORMATION)

"Start where you are. Use what you have. Do what you can." — Arthur Ashe

B efore we proceed, it's crucial that you fully grasp the scope and ultimate aim of the ICOR® Input stage.

Understanding the scope allows you to establish clear limits and boundaries, simplifying reality to make it more manageable, comprehensible, and ultimately, actionable.

The goal of this stage sharpens your focus, directing all your efforts toward specific achievements and stripping away any distractions, misunderstandings, or subjective interpretations.

In the Input stage, the goal is to capture information from two distinct sources: the Outer World and the Inner World, and integrate it into your productivity system.

Here's a quick breakdown:

- **Scope**. Gathering information from the Outer World and Inner World.
- **Goal**. Efficiently channeling the captured information from these sources into your productivity system.

You may now be asking, what exactly distinguishes the Outer World from the Inner World?

This is the perfect moment to delve into our first layer: concepts.

2.1.1 CONCEPTS

2.1.1.1 MASTERING THE SOURCES: HARNESSING INFORMATION FROM THE OUTER AND INNER WORLDS

"In the age of information, misinformation is the real enemy. It's crucial to verify sources and seek out multiple perspectives to truly understand the world around us." — Barack Obama

In any productivity system, you collect information from two different sources: the Outer World and the Inner World.

The Outer World includes information you encounter through external sources such as articles on the Internet, books, podcasts, or YouTube videos.

This information is created by others, not by you.

However, this doesn't prevent you from adding your own thoughts or annotations. For instance, you might jot down ideas or comments that strike you while consuming this content, which helps add personal context and understanding.

The Inner World, on the other hand, refers to information that originates directly from you, like your own thoughts or the notes you take during meetings.

Think of this as content where you are the creator or the "author." It springs from your own reflections and intellectual engagement.

Recognizing and distinguishing these sources intuitively is crucial because it influences the workflows and tools you choose to use. This distinction helps clarify common misunderstandings and confusions many busy professionals encounter in the realm of note-taking.

Now, let's dive deeper and define what effective note-taking really involves.

2.1.1.2 MASTERING THE ART OF NOTE-TAKING: ELEVATING INFORMATION INTO ACTION

"The discipline of writing something down is the first step toward making it happen." — Lee Iacocca

B efore we dive into the nuances of note-taking, let's begin with the basics: What exactly is a note?

By defining this clearly, we ensure that everyone is on the same page, fully understanding the concept behind the term.

Within the context of ICOR® and for busy professionals, we define a note as "a written record that captures important information, decisions, insights, or action items from various business-related activities."

Notes are crucial for recalling essential details, facilitating effective communication, and managing tasks efficiently.

It's important to note (pun intended) that when we say "written," we're not just referring to text. In today's digital age, notes can encompass a variety of formats, including images, audio recordings, videos, sketches, and more, all of which can be stored digitally.

Let's explore some practical examples to clarify this concept:

- **Meeting minutes**. These are formal records of the discussions, decisions, and assignments from business meetings.
- **Task lists**. These include actionable items identified during meetings or communications, complete with deadlines and priorities.
- **Client notes**. These capture crucial details from client interactions like preferences, feedback, and commitments.
- **Research notes**. These are summaries of key findings and insights from market research or data analysis.

- **Project notes**. These detail project statuses, challenges, next steps, and relevant updates for project management.
- **Ideas and brainstorming**. Notes from brainstorming sessions or personal creative thinking where new ideas and solutions are documented.
- **Training notes**. Key points from workshops, training sessions, or seminars that are applicable to professional development.
- **Conference and networking notes**. Important takeaways, contacts, and information gleaned from networking events and conferences.
- **Personal reflections and learning**. Notes on personal performance, goals, and insights crucial for one's professional growth.

These diverse scenarios underscore an important point: Notes can encapsulate both information and action, not merely passive data.

Understanding the dual foundations of information and action that ICOR® emphasizes, knowing what constitutes a note becomes straightforward.

Note-taking, then, can be described as "the art of capturing information from various sources in a manner that prepares you for remembering, comprehending, and most critically, taking action."

This is why note-taking is so essential, especially for busy professionals, as it becomes an essential tool in numerous business processes such as:

- **Retention**. Writing helps engage your senses, aiding memory retention and recall.
- **Understanding**. Taking notes often involves rephrasing and summarizing, deepening your understanding of the material.

- **Preparation**. Notes prepare you for communications and presentations, serving as structured references.
- **Documentation**. They provide a lasting record for future reference.
- **Analysis and critical thinking**. Effective note-taking involves processing information and making connections, enhancing your analytical skills.

To conclude, here are some strategies to enhance your note-taking:

- **Keep it clear and concise**. Focus on capturing essential points, action steps, and critical insights.
- **Structure is key**. Use templates or frameworks for consistent and easy retrieval.
- **Prioritize action items**. Emphasize decisions, tasks, deadlines, and follow-ups.
- **Integrate your tools**. Sync notes with additional software to streamline workflows.
- **Use visuals**. Use diagrams, flowcharts, and graphs to simplify complex information.
- **Highlight priorities**. Use colors, highlighting, or symbols to denote importance.
- **Reflect and analyze**. Don't just record facts. Include your insights and reflections to enrich decision-making and strategic planning.

With these practices, you can elevate your note-taking to become a pivotal element of your professional success.

2.1.1.3 FROM CLUTTER TO CLARITY: TRANSFORMING NOTE STORAGE FOR EFFECTIVE INFORMATION RETRIEVAL

"Simplicity is the ultimate sophistication." — Leonardo da Vinci

I f you're reading this book, chances are you're all too familiar with the chaos of disorganized notes: meeting notes scattered across your tablet, random thoughts captured on your phone, and perhaps even a sea of sticky notes engulfing your desktop.

And let's not even start on the frustration of searching for that one essential note amid the clutter, a search that often ends in stress and irritation.

To tackle this disarray, let's revisit a crucial concept introduced earlier in this book: the Single Source of Truth (SSOT).

This concept is your powerhouse tool for mastering the art of note-taking and indeed, it's a game changer for your overall productivity.

In note-taking, a SSOT acts as a specific, designated location where all your notes are systematically stored, making retrieval straightforward and stress-free. Imagine it as a well-organized library, where each book has a specific place on the shelf, easily locatable when needed.

However, this doesn't mean dumping all your notes into a single, massive container, the typical "one tool for everything" approach.

As we progress through this book, you'll see why the "one-size-fits-all" strategy doesn't quite work with software tools. Many busy professionals think that consolidating everything into one tool will simplify their lives, but in reality, this often leads to even more chaos.

It's important to remember that each tool is designed to address specific needs, not every possible scenario. If you're searching for a one-stop solution, you're likely on a path to disappointment because it's nearly impossible to find a tool that meets all needs.

Different types of notes require different tools, much like how various TV channels cater to specific interests. You wouldn't watch a nature documentary on a fashion channel, right?

As you capture information, whether from the Outer World or an idea that suddenly strikes coming from you Inner World, there are two key questions to help determine your SSOT:

- What type of note is this?
- Where would it make the most sense to find it later?

Also, think about your future self.

Take the time to name your notes wisely and add relevant context when storing them.

This little effort goes a long way in saving you future headaches, time, and even money when you need to retrieve that note. Essentially, you're laying out breadcrumbs for your future self to follow easily.

To enhance your note-storing process, consider using intermediate tools.

At the Paperless Movement®, we strive to minimize friction in all our workflows, believing that less friction translates to higher performance and less stress.

Sometimes, your SSOT might not be the most accessible tool in terms of friction. In such cases, it's practical to initially place your note in an easy-to-use intermediate tool. Later, when convenient, you can transfer it to the appropriate SSOT.

This method ensures a smooth, frictionless process, supporting the high-performance culture we advocate.

Let's look at an example to illustrate this point.

Suppose you've chosen a primary tool for your note-taking, but it falls short on mobile devices. You could opt for a tool that excels on mobile platforms, capturing information on the go with ease. Later, at your desktop, you can organize these notes from the mobile-friendly tool into your designated SSOT.

This approach lets you harness the strengths of different tools, avoiding their shortcomings and enhancing your productivity.

By leveraging the unique features of each tool, you achieve a seamless, high-performance workflow with minimal friction.

2.1.1.4 LINKING NOTES LIKE A PRO: MASTERING RETRIEVAL AND ORGANIZATION FOR PEAK PRODUCTIVITY

"A new idea is a combination of old elements." —James Webb Young

Once you've mastered capturing a note and storing it in the right place, its SSOT, it's crucial to think about how you can retrieve that information effortlessly and quickly.

There's a statistic out there (a research made by Asana, a Project Management tool) claiming busy professionals spend 60% of their time searching for information. We aim to drastically cut that down for you.

This is why it's essential to effectively link your notes, creating a system that makes retrieval easier. The better your notes are connected, the quicker and easier it is to pull that needed information when necessary.

We, as busy professionals, aren't buried in academia, dealing with vast PDFs and abstract concepts. Our needs are more straightforward.

We need to quickly access the meeting notes from a project, recall the name of a contact met at an event, or revisit the brilliant strategy we conceived while walking the dog.

Our challenges are numerous but practical, requiring rapid capture and retrieval to make the most of our time, as time literally translates to money for us.

Linking notes is about making connections that simplify recalling this information based on easily remembered details when you begin your search. Think of it as weaving a web of your notes, where instead of scattered thoughts, you have a robust network of interconnected information.

This workflow transforms your note management from merely jotting down to truly engaging with the world of information and knowledge. It's akin to moving from sticky notes strewn across your desk to a well-organized digital bulletin board.

And why, as a busy professional, should you link your notes? Here are several compelling reasons:

- **Seeing the big picture**. Linking notes helps you see how pieces of information fit together, offering a comprehensive view.
- **Brain-like connections**. Our brains naturally link ideas. By linking notes, you replicate this natural process, which is highly efficient. At the Paperless Movement®, we often say you have one brain with two parts: the physical and the digital. Making them work in harmony allows you to create and maintain the productivity system you've always wanted.
- **Quick access**. With linked notes, you can swiftly navigate through your productivity system and find what you need without wading through mountains of information.
- **Enhanced memory**. Linking notes engages your brain more deeply with the content, reinforcing memory.
- **Continuous learning**. As you link more information, your knowledge base expands and evolves.

However, as you delve deeper into the world of note-taking, you may encounter complex jargon like note-taking, note-making, links, backlinks, tags, etc. We aim to keep things simple, focusing on practical strategies that enhance your efficiency.

That's why we're breaking down five techniques into three manageable categories to help you link your notes in a breeze:

- Folders and tags.
- Links and backlinks.

- AI (Artificial Intelligence).

Many busy professionals, with the emergence of new Tools for Thought (TfT) or PKM (Personal Knowledge Management) tools, have overlooked the simplest approach: folders.

While some may view folders as old-fashioned, we believe in harnessing the strengths of all available strategies and techniques.

Folders help you categorize notes, which can be incredibly effective for those who need to find and retrieve information swiftly. Not all information needs to be interconnected; sometimes, it's useful to keep certain data isolated in a dedicated place where you know exactly where everything is.

For example, you might have all notes related to a specific project clearly separated and isolated. This organization not only makes it easy to locate the required information but also helps you stay focused and secure when accessing it.

However, every technique has its limitations. That's why we also advocate using tags, which allow you to label and identify notes across different folders.

Tags are a dynamic tool for labeling and identifying your notes, no matter where they are stored. This capability allows you to organize your notes into multiple folders while linking them through common tags.

For instance, if you assign the tag "productivity" to notes across different folders, a single search for this tag will pull up all related notes, irrespective of their physical location in your system.

This interconnected approach ensures that information is never isolated, making it easier for you to retrieve notes from anywhere in your storage system. While this sounds ideal, it's important to recognize that tags, like any technique, have their limitations.

Tags are incredibly flexible, allowing you to label notes liberally; for instance, as previously mentioned, tagging any relevant note with "productivity." However, this can lead to an overwhelming number of results when you search for this tag later, potentially cluttering your search instead of refining it.

Despite this, tags are pretty useful for many use cases.

They can be used to mark notes in different statuses. For example, by tagging them with "review," which later simplifies finding all notes that require your attention.

Another practical application is tagging notes with specific names of coworkers, which can be useful when you need to share information with colleagues without continuously interrupting them; just compile all the notes tagged with their names when you meet.

Moving beyond tags, we explore links and backlinks, key techniques in digital note-taking that enable you to create a structured, interconnected knowledge network.

Links, or forward links, help you navigate from one note to another seamlessly, much like hyperlinks on a webpage. For example, linking a person's name in a meeting note to a dedicated note about them makes it easy to access detailed information with a single click.

Backlinks, or incoming links, reveal all the notes that point to a particular note, offering a reverse view that can help you understand the broader context of information and how various notes are interconnected. This is particularly useful in managing complex projects or detailed profiles where understanding relational dynamics is key.

The advent of artificial intelligence (AI) has further revolutionized note-taking, introducing capabilities like auto-tagging through natural language processing. This means the system can automatically categorize a note as a "meeting" if it detects meeting-related content, reducing your manual tagging efforts.

Moreover, AI enhances the retrieval process through semantic search, which not only recognizes exact keywords but also understands related terms and contexts. For example, searching for "budget" might also bring up notes containing "cost" or related financial terms, immensely beneficial for quick data analysis and decision-making.

In conclusion, integrating various note-taking techniques (folders for categorization, tags for quick identification, links and backlinks for connectivity, and AI for intelligent processing) provides a comprehensive system that boosts efficiency, clarity, and productivity.

By leveraging each method's strengths, you can build a robust, easily navigable, and effective note-taking system that significantly enhances your professional workflows.

2.1.1.5 DECODING THE GOLDEN QUESTION: WHAT IS THE BEST NOTE-TAKING TOOL?

"You do not rise to the level of your goals. You fall to the level of your systems." — James Clear

We wrap up this section on concepts with a question frequently asked by busy professionals who are members of the Paperless Movement® Membership:

What is the best note-taking tool?

This question might seem logical, given your newfound awareness of how vital note-taking is to your workflow. You might believe that finding the perfect tool will streamline your processes and bring order to your work life, perhaps even providing an escape from the relentless pursuit of the ultimate note-taking solution.

However, we're here to tell you that this question, as it stands, is misguided. It's not framed correctly, which is why you've never found a satisfactory answer, and frankly, you never will.

Why is this the wrong question? There are two main reasons.

First, the type of content you're noting down matters. Different types of content may require different tools.

Second, the market is flooded with tools, each claiming supremacy. However, they serve varied purposes and comparing them directly without specific criteria is nonsense.

To help you understand better, here are some criteria you could consider when evaluating note-taking tools:

- **Storage**. Some tools like Logseq or Obsidian store information locally on your device, while others like Craft or Evernote use cloud storage.
- **Content creation**. There are tools designed for visual content like Miro, others that excel in outlining

like Roam, Tana, or Workflowy, and those better suited for long-form text like Heptabase. Within this category, some tools use Markdown, like Drafts, while others like Apple Notes use proprietary formats.

- **Organization**. Tools vary in how they organize or connect your notes; using folders, tags, links, backlinks, and even AI.
- **Connection level**. Some tools make connections at the note level, while others operate at the block level.
- **Target audience**. Tools like Obsidian might cater to developers with their extensive plugin features, while others like RemNote appeal to students or researchers with features supportive of methods like Zettelkasten.

Consider how many different tools we've just mentioned: more than ten! This illustrates the complexity of choosing the right tool.

Asking "What is the best note-taking tool?" is too broad and leads to confusion due to overlapping features among tools.

A better question would be: What is the best note-taking tool for the specific type of work I need to do?

Don't worry; we've done the heavy lifting for you in this book.

We've analyzed multiple scenarios that busy professionals encounter and have outlined efficient workflows and identified the best tools for each one of them.

Forget about comparing apples to oranges with questions like "Is Notion better than Evernote?" or "Should I use Obsidian over Tana?"

Instead, our approach focuses on specific concepts and workflows, and with the ICOR® Framework, you'll pinpoint the right tools for your needs and learn how to use them effectively.

We guarantee that you'll end up with the best tool stack you've ever had, tailored to function seamlessly with your cognitive processes.

That means zero friction and optimized productivity!

2.1.2 WORKFLOWS

2.1.2.1 MASTERING EFFICIENCY: A REVOLUTIONARY 6-WORKFLOW NOTE-TAKING SYSTEM FOR BUSY PROFESSIONALS

"If you can't describe what you are doing as a process, you don't know what you're doing." — W. Edwards Deming

We put a lot of thought into how to create a note-taking system tailored specifically to busy professionals like you.

We know your workdays are filled with meetings, projects, calls, and a constant flow of information, each demanding your attention. That's why we've crafted this note-taking system to meet your needs, providing practical advice and boosting your note-taking skills.

Forget about traditional methods like the Cornell Method or Zettelkasten. While they have their merits, they're not necessarily designed for busy professionals who need quick, actionable solutions.

Instead, we've reduced and simplified the world of note-taking into just six easy-to-follow workflows, each addressing a common scenario you're likely to encounter on a daily basis.

Here's an overview of these workflows, setting the stage for what you'll dive into next:

- **Workflow 1: The closest to paper experience**. This one is for those who crave the tactile feel of writing on paper. It's perfect for sketches and diagrams, offering a seamless transition from traditional to digital.
- **Workflow 2: Jot things down**. This is all about capturing quick thoughts, key information, or anything that pops up during your day. It's fast and flexible, keeping you from losing those sudden bursts of thoughts.
- **Workflow 3: Develop thinking**. When you need to create more detailed content, like presentations,

emails, articles, or defining a new product, strategy, or service, this workflow guides you through that process. It's great for personal reflection and strategic thinking.

- **Workflow 4: Writing and connecting information**. Designed for taking notes during meetings, online events, or phone calls, this workflow helps you keep track of important details and connect them with related information.
- **Workflow 5: Notes on third-party content**. This workflow focuses on taking notes from external sources, like websites, newsletters, PDFs, or YouTube videos. It helps you capture the valuable insights you gather from the outer world.
- **Workflow 6: The one that goes beyond**. This workflow takes your notes from mere information to action. It bridges the gap between information (knowledge) and action, helping you turn insights into tasks or projects, whether they belong to your personal or business (team) areas.

These six workflows cover just about every scenario a busy professional might face. Not only do they offer clear guidance on how to execute each workflow, step by step, but they also help you reduce the complexity of your note-taking process.

To help you even more, we've also designed the ICOR® Note-taking Framework, a tool you can use to map out your note-taking tool stack.

Just a heads-up: it's different from the ICOR® Framework, so don't mix them up!

The ICOR® Note-taking Framework is a circle divided into six areas, each representing a workflow. Each area is split into three levels (good, better, best) to show how effective each tool is for that specific workflow.

To use the ICOR® Note-taking Framework, you start by placing your current tools in the appropriate areas. Your goal is to fill the "best" areas for each workflow, ensuring you have the optimal tools for your note-taking system.

Once you've got all the "best" areas covered, you can look at reducing the number of tools you use by choosing versatile ones that cover multiple workflows.

For example, you might consider using the same tool for the "Jot things down," "Develop thinking," and "Writing/connecting information" workflows to simplify your note-taking tool stack.

With this framework, you'll be able to streamline your note-taking process and create a system that works for you, not against you. It's all about making sure your note-taking system serves a purpose, driving you toward your goals, not just piling up information.

We encourage you to explore the ICOR® Note-taking Framework by placing your current note-taking tools within it. If you need extra guidance, check out the Paperless Movement® website, where you'll find a video showing how to bring this concept to life.

Now that you have an overview of these workflows, let's dive into each one and explore how you can implement them to elevate your note-taking game.

2.1.2.2 WORKFLOW 1: THE CLOSEST TO PAPER EXPERIENCE

"Handwriting is more connected to the movement of the heart." — Natalie Goldberg

In this Information Management Era, driven by innovation, going paperless is a must for busy professionals. Yet, if you're among those who still cherish the tactile feel of writing on paper, the transition to digital can seem daunting.

Perhaps you've dabbled in multiple tools but found none of them quite capture the essence of pen and paper.

We get it, and that's why we've specifically created this workflow, where you'll learn the best practices you need to follow to make it work seamlessly.

Bet on this workflow to cover these needs: handwritten notes, sketching, or manually highlighting and annotating, always mimicking the paper experience.

Let's check the best practices you need to pay attention to:

- **Best practice 1: Define your goals**. Before you take the digital plunge, start by jotting down your goals. What do you hope to achieve by using this workflow? Is it reducing clutter, saving time, enhancing accessibility, or all of the above? Clarity on these goals will guide you in tailoring your new workflow.
- **Best practice 2: Equip yourself**. A successful transition begins with the right tools and accessories. We suggest using a tablet with a stylus, like an iPad with an Apple Pencil. The precision and responsiveness of an iPad could make you feel like writing on paper. To enhance the tactile experience, consider a paper-like screen protector. You might also want to check out e-ink devices designed for note-taking, like the reMarkable, Amazon Kindle Scribe, or

Boox.

- **Best practice 3: Select the right tools**. Choosing the right note-taking tool is critical. Each tool has its strengths and works best with certain types of notes. For this workflow, which emulates paper, consider tools like Apple Notes, GoodNotes, Notability, or Noteshelf. For simplicity and efficiency, as many times, our top pick is Apple Notes, as it covers a wide range of personal and business needs with minimal friction.
- **Best practice 4: Engage with your content**. Digital note-taking has the added advantage of interactivity. Highlight text, annotate PDFs, and even add multimedia elements to your notes. This step not only helps you engage more deeply with your content but also boosts comprehension and retention, encouraging you to finally move to the digital world of note-taking.
- **Best practice 5: Sync across devices**. One of the key benefits of going paperless is the ability to access your notes from anywhere. Make sure to sync your chosen tool across all your devices, ensuring your notes are always within reach.
- **Best practice 6: Organize your notes**. Digital notes can be organized in ways that paper can't match. Create virtual folders, use tags, and conduct quick text searches. No more rifling through piles of paper!

At this stage, it's crucial to revisit and internalize the concept of Single Source of Truth (SSOT).

Always remember this: Each of your notes should have a designated place where it ultimately resides (their SSOT), like meeting notes, personal thoughts, and so on.

The tools in this workflow are often intermediate steps before your notes reach their final SSOT. They offer the tactile sensations of physical paper without necessarily serving as the ultimate storage solution.

One final thought: Going paperless doesn't mean abandoning paper entirely. You can still use it for specific tasks or for its comfort factor. The key is integrating these physical elements into your digital workflow.

2.1.2.3 WORKFLOW 2: JOT THINGS DOWN

"The palest ink is better than the best memory." — *Chinese proverb*

T his workflow offers a simple and effective way to achieve peace of mind and regain control by capturing thoughts and ideas as they come.

By following this approach, you can quickly store in the right place any passing idea, ensuring nothing is lost while freeing up your mind to focus on more important tasks.

This workflow doesn't just keep you organized. It can also give you a burst of dopamine when you know your ideas are safely stored.

To get started with this workflow, consider asking yourself two questions whenever you have a new thought or idea:

1. Is this thought information or action?
2. Does this thought affect only me, or does it involve my team?

The order doesn't matter, and with practice, these questions will become second nature, with their answers coming to you almost simultaneously.

Why do these questions matter?

Because they guide you to our crucial and recurring concept of Single Source of Truth (SSOT).

Essentially, you need to quickly know where to store your thoughts, and answering these questions will help you do that efficiently without losing momentum.

Now, it's also the moment to use another helpful tool we've mentioned before: the ICOR® Framework.

Let's do some recap.

The ICOR® Framework not only helps you position your tools but also identifies four potential SSOTs to choose from: PKM, BKM, PPM, and BPM.

Here's a quick breakdown of what each one is for:

- **PKM (Personal Knowledge Management)** is for storing personal information; anything unique to you and not impacting anyone else.
- **BKM (Business Knowledge Management)** is for team-related information. Anything you need to share with your co-workers.
- **PPM (Personal Project Management)** is for managing your own tasks, the ones that only affect you..
- **BPM (Business Project Management)** is for tasks involving your team.

Let's simplify things by working backward from the end goal.

Always remember that your main goal is to quickly store the information or action from your thoughts in the right SSOT.

To do this, you need to figure out which of the four categories your thought fits into.

As you can see, it's really that straightforward: The answers to the two earlier questions will quickly point you to the right area of the ICOR® Framework and, consequently, the correct tool to use.

At this point, one important scenario to consider is whether you're in the office at your desktop or on the go with your mobile device.

On a desktop, it's easy to move ideas directly to their SSOT.

However, when you're on the move, the tools might not be as user-friendly, or you might just need to quickly jot down a thought in a rush.

This is where the intermediate tool, a concept we already mentioned in Workflow 1 ("The closest to paper experience"), comes into play again, serving as a temporary space for capturing notes and actions.

Later, you can process these notes and move them to the correct SSOT when you're back at your desktop, calmly drinking your cup of coffee.

By adopting this workflow, you'll be well on your way to achieving greater organization, focus, and productivity, ensuring not a single idea gets lost!

2.1.2.4 WORKFLOW 3: DEVELOP YOUR THINKING

"Clarity is the counterbalance of profound thoughts." —
Luc de Clapiers

T his workflow is crucial for busy professionals because it focuses on action, the driving force behind any successful productivity system.

Before we dive into the workflow, let's discuss the true purpose of note-taking and the broader note-taking landscape.

The ultimate goal of note-taking isn't just to accumulate notes. It should always lead to actions that help you achieve your goals.

Taking notes without translating them into action can create a false sense of productivity; it might feel like you're getting things done, but without action, you're just spinning your wheels.

This mindset can lead to stagnation in your Personal Knowledge Management (PKM) or Business Knowledge Management (BKM) systems. Action drives results, and without it, progress stalls, leaving you feeling stuck.

That's why this workflow is designed to ensure your note-taking process leads to tangible outcomes.

This workflow addresses two key business scenarios:

- **Crafting elaborate content**. Whether it's an email, a presentation, an article, or a report, this workflow guides you through the process of creating detailed and structured content.
- **Promoting and encouraging self-reflection**. This aspect focuses on fostering strategic thinking and personal development.

To achieve these goals, you'll need the right tools, which can be categorized into three types:

- **Visual tools**. These are great for mind mapping and diagramming, helping you visually organize complex ideas and create connections between them. Popular tools include MindNode and Miro.
- **Outliners**. Tools like Roam, Workflowy, Tana, RemNote, or Logseq are designed for creating structured lists and hierarchies. This structure brings clarity to your thoughts and allows you to take action.
- **Journaling tools**. Journaling tools like Day One or Stoic are perfect for personal reflection and capturing daily thoughts, whether work-related or personal.

To use these tools effectively, always consider what types of processes they are best suited for:

- **Visual tools**. Ideal for dealing with complex content, they allow you to use shapes, arrows, and diagrams to map out your thoughts. This visual approach helps transform chaos into coherence, providing a bird's-eye view of your ideas, making it easier to take action on them.
- **Outliners**. They are perfect for organizing thoughts into hierarchical structures, bringing clarity and logic to your thinking. These tools make it easy to create, edit, and rearrange information, helping you understand complex ideas. Simplicity opens the door to action.
- **Journaling tools**. These are excellent for personal reflection and strategic thinking, offering a wide-open space for free expression, which can lead to new insights and creativity.

This workflow, "Develop your thinking," helps you create structured and impactful content by leveraging the tools best suited for the task.

It's about building a process that fosters creativity, strategic thinking, and personal growth while ensuring nothing falls through the cracks, whether it's about expressing your ideas or building a productivity system that encourages action.

Remember, action is the ultimate goal of note-taking. If your notes don't lead to action, it's time to reconsider your approach.

In the Control stage of ICOR®, we'll dive deeper into how you can turn your information into action.

2.1.2.5 WORKFLOW 4: WRITE AND CONNECT INFORMATION

"Great things are not done by impulse, but by a series of small things brought together." — Vincent Van Gogh

I n this chapter, we explore a common challenge that busy professionals like you face every day: effectively capturing notes that are directly relevant to the activities you're engaged in.

Unlike the spontaneous note-taking discussed in Workflow 2, this approach focuses on actively recording information during live situations: meetings, events, or phone calls.

The goal here is not just to take notes but to integrate them seamlessly into your existing note-taking system, enhancing your ability to connect and retrieve information when needed.

To streamline this process, we've divided note-taking tools into two primary categories:

1. Text-Focused tools.

These tools are primarily designed for handling text and often use Markdown, a user-friendly markup language that helps format text simply. Within this category, there are two types of tools:

- **Manual Tools**. These require you to manually link your notes by adding tags or creating hyperlinks. These tools, while offering significant flexibility, demand manual effort to establish these connections.
- **AI-based Tools**. Leveraging artificial intelligence, these tools automatically forge links among your notes. These tools reduce your workload by intuitively suggesting connections and associations, freeing you from manual linking tasks.

2. Tools for multiple formats.

Moving beyond plain text, these tools support rich formatting options (multiple fonts, colors, highlights, and so forth).

Clear examples include Microsoft Word, Google Docs, Evernote, or Craft.

They excel in versatility, providing an amazing user experience across all devices, be it smartphones, tablets, or desktop computers. Despite some critics labeling them as "old school," their intuitive design and adaptability make them a great bet for non-nerdy busy professionals.

A crucial aspect of mastering this workflow is maintaining a reliable Single Source of Truth (SSOT) for your notes.

Just as in previous workflows, if you find yourself mobile and the tool at hand isn't optimal, you can use an intermediate tool to capture the information. Later, you can process these notes and integrate them into your SSOT.

Once your notes are securely stored in your SSOT, you may add manual connections, like tags or links, as necessary. If you're using an AI-based tool, it will handle these connections for you, simplifying your workflow.

Consider tags and links as essential tools for structuring your notes in a way that enhances future access and retrieval. We highly recommend connecting your notes to relevant projects, tasks, or individuals involved.

An innovative feature in this workflow is the use of transcription tools for online meetings.

These tools not only transcribe and summarize discussions but also highlight conclusions and suggest follow-up actions. They prove invaluable by allowing you to be focused on the conversation, eliminating the need to take detailed notes manually; a significant point for busy professionals.

With this workflow, you are equipped to develop a more organized, efficient, and interconnected note-taking system, enabling you to manage information more effectively and boost your productivity.

2.1.2.6 WORKFLOW 5: NOTE-TAKING ON THIRD PARTY CONTENT

"Your mind is for having ideas, not holding them." — *David Allen*

T his workflow is fully-focused on the Outer World and how you can take notes based on the vast ocean of information you encounter daily, as you navigate a virtual tsunami of content coming from all directions: articles, YouTube videos, newsletters, brochures, PDF documents, emails, and more.

Imagine if you could master this chaos.

What if you could turn this flood of information into a well-organized flow of valuable knowledge?

This is the ultimate goal of this workflow: to develop a robust note-taking system that enables you to efficiently organize and store each piece of information in a designated Single Source of Truth (SSOT).

And, to do so, the first step is to implement a pause, a moment to collect and centralize the information before deciding its final destination.

Enter the "read-later" tools, such as Readwise Reader App or Matter. These tools act as a holding area, providing a space to pause and evaluate the captured information. Here, you can sift through the incoming information, deciding what's truly valuable and distinguishing it from mere noise.

It's important to recognize not everything capturing your attention initially needs to be preserved. You need to differentiate between signal and noise.

With a read-later tool, you have the luxury of time to carefully assess, highlight crucial points, tag, and annotate.

Later, you can transfer only the most pertinent insights

into your SSOT, ensuring that your digital repository is both relevant and manageable.

Additionally, there are tools tailored for specific types of content. For instance, PDF readers, like PDF Expert, excel at emulating the experience of interacting with physical documents.

You can annotate, highlight, and even doodle in the margins just as you would on paper.

These annotations can then be seamlessly exported into your SSOT, providing easy access and reference.

By integrating these tools into your workflow, you regain control over your digital environment, transforming potential chaos into a curated collection of insights that enhance your productivity and knowledge management.

2.1.2.7 WORKFLOW 6: THE ONE THAT GOES BEYOND

"Once we accept our limits, we go beyond them." — *Albert Einstein*

We call this workflow "The one that goes beyond" because it literally extends well beyond traditional note-taking by addressing two crucial scenarios for any busy professional:

1. Creating a personal or business Knowledge Management system.
2. Moving and translating information into action.

The true value of your notes lies in their transformation into knowledge.

This conversion, which we could consider an action itself, clarifies and processes the information you've captured, enabling you to shift from mere information to knowledge and, consequently, actionable insights.

This is what makes this workflow so essential: it turns scattered, isolated, or otherwise meaningless information into tangible outcomes.

It not only enhances your understanding of the information (that's why we call it knowledge) but also outlines clear actions you can take and complete, helping you move closer to your goals.

In our ICOR® Framework, we represent this concept with its four main areas, each blending knowledge and action. This structure highlights potential overlaps and guides you in choosing the right tools for each purpose:

- **PKM**: Personal Knowledge Management.
- **BKM**: Business Knowledge Management.
- **PPM**: Personal Project Management (also known as Task Management).

- **BPM**: Business Project Management.

Each area could be supported by tools that may first appear as note-taking tools but actually offer much more.

Take Notion, for instance.

Describing Notion merely as a note-taking tool would be akin to calling a smartphone just a phone. Notion offers relational databases and team collaboration features, making it a powerhouse for both personal and business Knowledge Management.

Another example is ClickUp, which perfectly merges Knowledge Management with Project Management.

It transitions seamlessly from information to action, embodying the essence of this workflow.

So, what are the steps to follow within this workflow?

The process could mirror earlier workflows we've discussed but with a focus on linking notes to actions.

You might start by capturing notes in an intermediate, mobile-friendly tool, if necessary like, for example, Apple Notes, that feels natural to you.

Later, when you have time, you'd transfer these notes to Notion, ClickUp, or another designated Single Source of Truth (SSOT). Here, you delve deeper into the content, converting it into knowledge or directly crafting actions that need to be executed.

By adhering to this workflow, you not only push yourself and your notes towards actionable outcomes, the ultimate aim, but also ensure your note-taking system maximizes its potential.

A robust note-taking system does more than store information; it facilitates easy retrieval and conversion into meaningful actions, providing a clear path for evolving your notes into action items (tasks or projects), and ultimately, completed goals.

2. 2 STAGE 2: CONTROL (INFORMATION)

"All life is problem solving." — Karl Popper

We concluded the ICOR® Input stage with a final workflow we call "The one that goes beyond."

This workflow seamlessly leads us into the gateway to ICOR®'s next stage: Control.

As we've mentioned earlier, Control is all about transforming captured information into actionable knowledge.

Working and engaging with this information is an action in itself, as it allows us to delve deeper, identifying gaps and redundancies, and bringing order to chaos. This clarity fosters understanding, an invaluable outcome in any productivity system.

Don't think of understanding in the same way you did back in school or university. You're not a PhD crafting a thesis. As a busy professional, understanding takes on a completely different meaning and requires a distinctly practical approach.

To better illustrate this concept, consider you're working on your business strategy.

The moment you truly "understand" your strategy is the moment a clear path to your goals emerges. This epiphany allows you to transition from raw information to well-defined actions, which we will structure using our Output Elements, entities we'll describe later in this book.

Think of the Control stage of ICOR® as a strategic moment to reflect on how to handle information, from both your Inner and Outer worlds, with the sole purpose of taking effective action. Be ruthless in this approach: Information without action is simply nonsense and a complete waste of time.

Don't be satisfied just because your productivity system is overflowing with information.

You know better than anyone that merely capturing and storing data or information for its own sake can be frustrating, overwhelming, and ultimately pointless. True satisfaction only comes from taking decisive action, completing tasks, and ultimately achieving your goals.

Starting with the end in mind allows you to reverse engineer the steps you need to take with your information.

The key is this: building a practical and fully-functional PKM (Personal Knowledge Management) system begins even before you start capturing information. It starts with cutting down on the overwhelming flood of information you face daily in the Outer World (emails, social media, YouTube videos, podcasts, blog posts, direct messages, notifications...), streamlining what truly deserves your attention.

That's why we developed a mental model we will deeply describe later on called The Capturing Beast, a workflow entirely focused on managing your attention.

By implementing The Capturing Beast, you'll achieve our ultimate goal in the Control stage: to help you concentrate on crucial information, allowing you to navigate through the chaos of the Outer World without feeling lost or overwhelmed.

You'll learn to focus on information that aligns with your goals, transforming it into actions that propel your projects forward and help you achieve them.

By fully integrating The Capturing Beast into your routine, you've taken a significant step toward creating your ideal PKM system, a key component of any productivity system, as it sets the stage for everything that follows.

This approach will blend smoothly into your productivity

system, allowing you to run your PKM system on autopilot, effortlessly. This is always the ultimate goal of any system: to minimize the energy you expend in its operation.

This is how you create a system you can trust; one that provides the control and peace of mind you need to consistently excel, day in and day out, without excuses.

Now, let's delve into the key concepts that will help you establish a solid foundation for your productivity system. We'll break these down one by one!

2.2.1 CONCEPTS

2.2.1.1 DEMYSTIFYING PKM: UNDERSTANDING PERSONAL KNOWLEDGE MANAGEMENT AND PKM SYSTEMS

"An investment in knowledge pays the best interest." —
Benjamin Franklin

B efore we dive into designing or conceptualizing your Personal Knowledge Management (PKM) system, it's essential to clearly define what PKM really means. This way, we make sure we're all on the same page, with a shared understanding and a clear vision, keeping our goals aligned as we proceed to design and build your productivity system.

Personal Knowledge Management, or PKM, is more than an abstract concept. It's an evolving process that encompasses the discovery, capture, and processing of information. This process is essential to generate actionable steps that drive you towards your goals.

However, PKM extends beyond these foundational elements.

It also involves critical intermediate steps like structuring and linking ideas, which are essential for deep understanding. This depth of understanding is what enables the formulation of truly impactful actions.

A well-crafted PKM system does more than just facilitate the mechanics of Knowledge Management. It actively fosters and enhances it.

It becomes an indispensable part of your workflow, seamlessly integrating into how you operate and clearly influencing your thought process. Remember, the tools we shape end up shaping us in return.

In this section, we introduce a PKM system that is far from a mere repository for ideas. It is a dynamic tool crafted to refine your thoughts, prompt necessary actions, and expedite your success. Imagine it as a machine that thrives on a positive feedback loop, increasing in efficiency with each use.

The more streamlined and intuitive the system, the faster and smoother your progress, accelerating the achievement of your goals. Failing to harness the full potential of our systems means missing out on significant enhancements to our work and outcomes.

Our systems are designed to be self-sustaining "living creatures," minimizing effort while maximizing satisfaction and results.

After all, if they didn't markedly improve our efficiency and outcomes, what would be the point of developing them?

2.2.1.2 THE GAME-CHANGER FOR BUSY PROFESSIONALS: WHY YOU NEED A PKM SYSTEM

"One cannot think without writing." — Niklas Luhmann

A s a busy professional, grasping the "Why" behind any endeavor is crucial before you commit your time, money, and resources. This understanding not only guides your decisions but also fuels your motivation to take action.

This is precisely why we're going to explore four fundamental "Why's" that illustrate the significant impact a well-designed Personal Knowledge Management (PKM) system can have on your work and life.

The PKM system we're about to introduce isn't just theoretical; it's the same system we, at the Paperless Movement®, use daily.

Developed through decades of productivity expertise, this system operates seamlessly, enhancing our business and personal lives, and we believe it can transform yours too.

Understanding and implementing an effective PKM system is vital for optimizing your professional and personal activities.

Let's dive into the first "Why."

Consider this insight from Sönke Ahrens in his book How to Take Smart Notes: "Every intellectual endeavor starts with a note."

This simple truth underscores the importance of capturing every fleeting idea or complex project detail.

A solid PKM system ensures that no idea is lost, maximizing the potential of each thought. It aids in assessing the value of these ideas, helping you decide which to pursue and which to discard.

Imagine possessing such clarity: How transformative could

that be for you?

The second "Why" revolves around two key principles: leverage and compounding.

Albert Einstein famously remarked, "Compound interest is the eighth wonder of the world. He who understands it, earns it; he who doesn't, pays it."

This principle also applies to knowledge.

You can either rush on a shaky foundation or build gradually on a solid base of understanding.

A PKM system amplifies your efforts by storing ideas and fostering connections, gradually building a robust knowledge base that propels you toward your goals, spurs serendipitous discoveries, and maintains a clear focus to boost your productivity and momentum.

Our third "Why" focuses on the power of reflection.

Often underestimated, the act of thinking and reflecting is crucial in determining success or failure. It's not just our experiences that shape us, but our reflections on them.

Deliberating on the underlying thoughts behind your actions can profoundly influence your career and life.

With deeper understanding comes fewer setbacks and frustrations.

By investing time in thoughtful reflection, you enhance your decision-making skills, significantly increasing your likelihood of success. A well-crafted PKM system not only facilitates thinking: it actively encourages it!

Finally, the ultimate "Why:" transitioning from passive information consumption to active implementation.

Reflect on this: How often do you actively use the information you acquire?

In an era teeming with information, mere access is insufficient: action is essential.

Consider the words of James Dyson, founder of Dyson Ltd.: "Perhaps millions of people, over the last few thousand years, have had ideas for improving [things]. All I did was take things a little further than just having the idea."

Dyson exemplifies the importance of action.

So, why delay building a system that effectively addresses all these "Why's"?

Let's start this journey together, transforming how you engage with information and ideas, ensuring they lead to meaningful action.

2.2.1.3 BRAIN POWER: LEVERAGING SHALLOW AND DEEP THINKING FOR SUCCESS

"You have to work hard to get your thinking clean to make it simple. But it's worth it in the end, because once you get there, you can move mountains." — Steve Jobs

In exploring the realm of thinking within any PKM system, it's pivotal to recognize two distinct types of thinking processes: Shallow Thinking and Deep Thinking.

Gaining insight into these processes not only enhances our understanding of mental activities but also improves how we manage our PKM system and select the appropriate tools for each type of thinking.

Shallow Thinking revolves around the swift capture and retrieval of information. It represents the preliminary layer of our thought process, where information is processed almost instantaneously.

For organizing this information, simple methods like tagging or basic categorization can be employed.

Some professionals go a step further by integrating AI tools or automated algorithms to streamline this process, thereby saving time and enhancing access to information.

It's crucial for busy professionals to value Shallow Thinking highly; despite its name, it plays a central role in managing the demanding pace of our daily routines.

Neglecting to process the vast amounts of Shallow Thinking required daily can lead to overwhelming backlogs, crucial for keeping our operations running smoothly.

Therefore, we need efficient workflows and tools that allow for the quick processing of such thoughts or ideas; be it meeting notes, impromptu thoughts during a call, or urgent tasks that must not be overlooked.

Conversely, Deep Thinking delves into a more profound layer

of our cognitive process.

This is where significant development and understanding happens.

Deep Thinking involves dissecting concepts, synthesizing ideas, and exploring them thoroughly to unearth meaningful insights and solutions. It goes beyond superficial knowledge, striving for a deep comprehension of the underlying aspects.

Visualization is a powerful tool in Deep Thinking. As visual beings, we find that seeing the comprehensive picture aids in grasping complex ideas more effectively. Through visualization, we identify gaps, derive meaning, and elevate our thinking to new levels.

However, to fully harness the depth of our explorations, visualization must be complemented with detailed written content, especially when we venture deep into topics crucial for achieving our goals.

By distinguishing between Shallow and Deep Thinking, you not only comprehend the various phases of the thinking process but also the most suitable tools for each phase.

This awareness helps you identify when you are engaged in either type of thinking, allowing you to manage your mental load more effectively and reduce stress by clearly understanding your current focus and goals.

2.2.1.4 DECODING CONTEXT: THE KEY TO SEAMLESS KNOWLEDGE MANAGEMENT AND ENHANCED PRODUCTIVITY

"In the digital era, context and connection are more important than ever before." —John Seely Brown

I f you've delved into PKM, you've likely encountered a key concept repeatedly: context.

This term pops up so frequently it can leave many scratching their heads.

Our goal here is to clarify this concept, drawing clear lines to ensure it enhances your productivity system effectively.

Traditionally, PKM systems have you categorize information into specific topics. This often leads to folders or tags like "productivity," which quickly become cluttered with countless ideas. A chaotic jumble that overwhelms the brain and hinders efficient processing.

Context is often mystifying, not least because some experts or "productivity gurus" suggest defining it by asking: In which future scenario will I want to revisit this idea?

But let's face it, when you capture and store an idea, it's usually impossible to predict when you'll want to access it again, right?

It's time to reimagine context to make it more practical, consistent, and intuitive.

For our purposes, understanding context involves two key actions:

1. **Tracing**. Identify the origin (source) of the information. Was it from a tweet, a meeting, an article, or a specific event? Pinning down as many details as possible makes it easier to retrieve this information later because your brain thrives on detailed context.
2. **Integrating**. This is about weaving the new information into your existing knowledge base in a way

that makes sense to you.

To facilitate these actions, we'll introduce a concept called Bucket, which we'll explore in more detail soon.

When you capture something new, your immediate tasks are to trace and integrate this information, ideally, on autopilot.

Why rely on solid tools for this process? Because understanding and internalizing your gathered information is crucial.

When you understand something thoroughly, it naturally stimulates your thinking process. This is pivotal because understanding leads to organic contemplation.

You begin to think about the information subconsciously, which then propels you towards action; whether that's implementing ideas, dismissing them as irrelevant, or saving them for future use.

By mastering the art of tracing and integrating, you set the stage for deeper understanding and more effective Knowledge Management.

This not only makes your thought process more fluid but also ensures that each piece of information serves a purpose, enhancing your overall productivity and clarity.

2.2.1.5 INBOX MASTERY: TURNING A DUMPING GROUND INTO A PRODUCTIVITY HUB

"Wisdom is knowing what to do next; Skill is knowing how to do it, and Virtue is doing it." — David Starr Jordan

W e'd like to draw your attention to a pivotal concept that's essential for crafting a productivity system that operates seamlessly, allowing you to perform at your best without the risk of burnout.

If you grasp and internalize this concept thoroughly, you'll be well-equipped to design and build the productivity system you've always envisioned.

This concept is a cornerstone, foundational to everything we discuss about productivity.

Understanding what an inbox is gets you halfway to success.

The other half?

Learning how to make an inbox work for you, rather than against you, a common struggle for many.

Over the years, we've engaged with countless busy professionals, exchanging insights on productivity and helping them to become more productive. These discussions have revealed a frequent misunderstanding of the concept "inbox," leading many to miss out on its substantial benefits.

Your PKM system is no different.

We stress this point: Adept use of inboxes can dramatically boost productivity, reduce stress, and help manage your tasks efficiently.

Why?

Because inboxes are at the core of effective productivity systems. A solid foundation here makes all the difference.

However, inboxes often face criticism and misuse. They

become dumping grounds for tasks or pieces of information, transforming your productivity system into a cluttered mess. This creates the dreaded "monster task" of inbox processing, where organizing takes precedence over doing.

To dispel any misconceptions, let's clarify what an inbox is not.

It is not merely a placeholder for delaying tasks or a temporary cache for ideas that interrupts workflow. It is much more significant than that.

At ICOR®, we often return to a fundamental concept introduced at the start of this book: the Single Source of Truth (SSOT). Remember this: the SSOT principle involves storing everything in its rightful place, enabling you to retrieve it intuitively and effortlessly later on.

An inbox becomes crucial when the SSOT is not immediately clear. It provides a moment to consider where something should ultimately live and be stored. This is particularly useful when you cannot directly store an item in its designated SSOT.

In high-pressure situations, typical in our daily professional lives, placing an item in the inbox allows you to momentarily free your mind, secure in the knowledge that it will be handled correctly later.

So, what exactly is an inbox? How could we define it?

An inbox is a temporary SSOT used when you cannot immediately direct an item to its final SSOT, its final destination.

Items should not linger in the inbox; ideally, clearing it should take no longer than five minutes. To achieve this, process your inbox daily to keep the workload manageable.

Inbox processing involves evaluating each item and relocating it to the appropriate SSOT without delay.

We will delve deeper into this process in the upcoming chapters, particularly as we explore the Task Management system.

Here, at the Paperless Movement®, we've relied on inboxes for decades to streamline our workflows.

Their significance is underscored by their inclusion as a standard feature in most productivity tools on the market, designed with busy professionals in mind.

It's up to you whether to use inboxes in your productivity system, but we really suggest you consider their huge value.

Getting to know and using inboxes can make a big difference in your daily life, since they're a key starting point for building any solid productivity system and are intrinsically related to the core concept of a system.

Trust us on this!

2.2.1.6 ORGANIZE LIKE A PRO: DIFFERENTIATING BETWEEN BUCKETS AND INBOXES

"We do not learn from experience. We learn from reflecting on experience." — John Dewey

At first glance, distinguishing between an inbox and a bucket might seem confusing, but fear not; we're here to clarify the difference.

Think of a bucket as a repository. It provides a context for storing ideas, making it easier to retrieve and understand complex topics later on. Unlike an inbox, a bucket doesn't press you to take immediate action on the contents you store there.

Conversely, an inbox demands your attention and regular processing, as we mentioned earlier. The primary function of an inbox is to house items that need prompt action. Essentially, you should aim to process your inbox until it's empty.

Now, a bucket is different. Its main goal isn't to incite action, but to support it when necessary.

This might seem like a subtle distinction, but as you delve deeper into this book, you'll discover that crafting an effective productivity system hinges on recognizing and leveraging these subtle nuances. Each nuance contributes to the system's overall value.

So, please pay close attention to these subtleties, as they are where the real value lies.

To better understand the roles of an inbox and a bucket, let's consider a practical example: Imagine an idea strikes you; an idea that at first seems game-changing (as they always appear to be at first...).

You're faced with two choices:

1. **The idea doesn't require immediate action**: simply

store it in a bucket, adding enough context to ensure it's easily accessible when needed in the future.

2. **The idea demands action**: place it in your inbox. This allows you the space to calmly analyze and decide on the necessary steps. Once processed, if the idea still holds relevance but no immediate action is needed, you might transfer it to a bucket.

Envision buckets as either broad or specific storage spaces for your accumulated knowledge, like categories for major topics that interest you or bins for particular projects you are actively working on.

By grasping the distinct functions of buckets and inboxes, you're setting the stage for a more organized and productive approach to handling information and action.

2.2.2 WORKFLOWS

"If you spend too much time thinking about a thing, you'll never get it done." — Bruce Lee

This is the moment where we dive deeper into the essential steps for getting your PKM system up and running. Yes, it's a pivotal moment. In fact, believe us: it's a life-changing one!

Whenever you encounter significant moments in life, you first need to envision them. In this case, you need to visualize the system we aim to build to make it a reality.

This system is ambitious because it needs to be intuitive and seamless, guiding you effortlessly, with zero friction and on autopilot, from one step to the next, following the natural course of your thought process.

This is where you'll see how the concepts we've explained before come to life. They'll help you connect the dots, creating a natural understanding of what a PKM system is and how it fits seamlessly into your current productivity system.

To make this system a reality, we'll describe, step by step, a crucial workflow named The Knowledge Management Cycle.

This cycle consists of five sequential stages, each essential to ensuring that your PKM system doesn't just store information but propels you into action. With The Knowledge Management Cycle, you'll ensure every captured piece of information aligns with your goals and interests.

Beyond just collecting data, this cycle pushes you to act on the information, which involves:

1. Reflecting on it.
2. Diving deeper into its nuances.
3. Taking tangible actions towards your goals.

To better understand The Knowledge Management Cycle, we'll divide it into sequential stages:

1. Discover
2. Capture
3. Process
4. Act
5. Share

But, before we dive into each of these stages, we will explain a mental model we've designed to enhance this cycle: The Capturing Beast.

This mental model will literally revolutionize how you approach the world of information.

2.2.2.1 THE ART OF SELECTIVE ATTENTION: EMBRACE THE CAPTURING BEAST

"People who can quickly distinguish what matters from what doesn't gain a huge advantage in a world where the flow of information never stops." — Shane Parrish

F rom now on, we want you to transform the way you face and handle information.

As a busy professional, you're bombarded with information every day. Sorting through what's important and what's not can be overwhelming, especially when you're battling the fear of missing out (FOMO).

Yes, today we're exposed to an overwhelming amount of information. We often think it's all crucial, believing any of it could literally "change our lives." We don't want to miss out, but trying to absorb it all is impossible.

That's where The Capturing Beast comes in. It helps you focus on the information that truly matters, ensuring you're not missing anything important while avoiding FOMO.

Before diving into this mental model, let's ease the pressure with a bold statement:

"Even if you stopped consuming all new information from now on, you could still live a meaningful life."

Embracing this simplicity paves the way for focus, which is key to peak performance. By understanding this, you release the pressure to constantly consume information.

Remember, you're already in a fantastic position in both work and life, and information is just a tool to help you grow even further.

The Capturing Beast is a mental model designed to help you identify relevant information, guiding you towards peace of mind. Think of it as an "attention mental model" aimed at pinpointing what you need to focus on and letting go of the rest.

The Capturing Beast consists of three layers:

1. Current Projects.
2. Key Elements (KEs).
3. Topics.

Each layer acts as a filter, highlighting what deserves your attention. Anything that doesn't pass through these filters is not worth your time.

Now, let's break it down!

If you want to build a PKM system focused on action to achieve your goals, your Current Projects are key.
Later in this book, we'll define what a Project is in detail, but for now, think of projects as containers for all the tasks needed to achieve a specific goal you've set.

When you're faced with new information, the first filter to use is this:

- Is this information directly relevant to my Current Projects?
- Does it impact the actions I need to take to achieve my goals?

If the answer is yes, pay attention to it. If not, let it go.

For example, imagine you're working on a project to build a new product for your company.

If you come across a blog post outlining the ten steps to building a successful product, or a YouTube video where Elon Musk discusses product design, this information should immediately resonate with you. Take the time to capture it. You can decide later if you need to delve deeper.

By focusing only on information that impacts your Current Projects, you ensure that it will drive you to take action and enhance or support those projects.

Just this first filter (Current Projects) alone can bring clarity to the overwhelming amount of information out there.

But The Capturing Beast doesn't stop here.

The next layer to filter information is through Key Elements.

Key Elements are the essential aspects of your life that need your attention, such as your company, your business partner, or your health. Any piece of information that impacts these Key Elements deserves your focus.

For instance, if you come across something interesting for your company, it's worth paying attention to.

Similarly, if you find an article that might benefit your business partner, take a few moments to check it out.

Finally, we come to the third and last way of filtering information with The Capturing Beast: Topics.

These are subjects you're interested in exploring further, such as your hobbies or anything relevant to your business or personal life: communication strategies, marketing, decision-making processes, you name it.

You can easily think of dozens or even hundreds of Topics, but this can be overwhelming and counterproductive. That's why we recommend limiting your focus to just three Topics at a time. You can review and adjust these Topics whenever you like, for example, monthly, quarterly, or even yearly. It's up to you.

The goal is to make significant progress by dedicating your attention to these main Topics. For example, if you choose CRM (Customer Relationship Management) tools as one of your topics, focus on it for an entire quarter.

By doing so, you'll gather valuable information, proactively seek out resources, process and understand it better, and ultimately achieve tangible results.

This approach ensures that the time and energy you invest lead to meaningful outcomes, rather than feeling like you're spinning your wheels.

This doesn't mean you should not store anything at all related to other Topics outside of the three you're focused on. The point is not dedicating a lot of time to them. You just store them and keep focusing your efforts on the three main Topics you've bet on during the time period you've decided.

Now, try looking at the world through the three layers of The Capturing Beast to determine what information deserves your attention.

By focusing on your current Projects, Key Elements, and three chosen Topics, you'll have more than enough to work with while dramatically reducing the scope of your attention. Setting these boundaries makes information more manageable and actionable.

Information will now help you to:

- Complete your current Projects and reach your goals.
- Focus on the essential aspects of your work and life (Key Elements).
- Dive deeper into subjects (Topics) that intrigue you.

When facing new information, always ask:

- Is it relevant to my current Projects?
- Is it crucial for any of my Key Elements?
- Does it relate to the three Topics I've chosen to explore this quarter?

Master this approach, and you'll become a true "capturing beast!"

Once you've reframed your attention, you're ready to enter The Knowledge Management Cycle.

2.2.2.2 STAGE 1: DISCOVER

"Knowledge wants to talk. Wisdom wants to listen." —
Haemin Sunim

E xploring new information can be both captivating and enlightening. It introduces you to fresh perspectives, diverse worlds, and unique experiences.

When delving into the stage of discovery, you typically encounter two ways to find information: intentionally and accidentally.

Intentional discovery happens when you have a specific goal in mind. You actively seek out information on purpose, diving deep with a focused target.

This approach is the easiest because it provides clarity, acting as a shield against the relentless stream of information you're bombarded with daily.

Accidental discovery, on the other hand, occurs when information presents itself unexpectedly, at any moment and in any place.

This is why we've transitioned from the Information Era to the Information Management Era. Accessing information isn't the challenge anymore; managing it is!

To navigate this sea of information, you need strategies to protect yourself from overload and identify what truly matters. This is where the mental model we've previously shared, The Capturing Beast, comes to your rescue.

The Capturing Beast helps you end up in the same place as intentional discovery, allowing you to grow your knowledge purposefully instead of being swept away by the turbulent river of random information.

It helps you prioritize, so you can focus on what genuinely

aligns with your current needs and circumstances based on your current Projects, Key Elements, and main Topics.

From this point, you can easily transition to the second stage of The Knowledge Cycle: Capture.

2.2.2.3 STAGE 2: CAPTURE

"Learning never exhausts the mind." — *Leonardo da Vinci*

One of the key concepts we've discussed before is the inbox. It's a simple yet powerful technique to boost your productivity.

Rule number one: whenever you come across something noteworthy, send it to an inbox immediately. Think of it like being on autopilot.

You can have multiple inboxes. We recommend starting with two: one for the Outer World and another for your Inner World.

It may seem too simple, but this setup is incredibly effective. It brings clarity to your productivity system and helps you design workflows that you can easily implement.

Here's how it works:

1. **Outer World inbox**. This is where you capture anything from the external environment. We recommend using a read later app for this purpose.
2. **Inner World inbox**. This is for your own thoughts and ideas. Most note-taking tools have an inbox feature where you can store items to process later.

Why use this inbox approach?

1. **Reduces FOMO**. By easily capturing the things that resonate with you, you release the tension and pressure of missing out (FOMO).
2. **Buys thinking time**. Inboxes create a pause between capturing and processing content.
3. **Enhances decision-making**. Inboxes help you assess the importance of information and decide whether to act on it or simply forget about it.

This workflow may seem slow or tedious at first, but starting small is crucial. Don't worry at this moment. You'll quickly adapt and find ways to streamline the workflow using your common sense.

Right now, speed isn't your priority. Clarity is. It's the key ingredient to designing your ideal workflow and PKM system.

2.2.2.4 STAGE 3: PROCESS

"What we think, we become." — Buddha

A solid PKM system is key to distinguishing valuable information (signal) from the unimportant (noise).

Using the Process stage in your PKM system allows you to filter your inboxes effectively.

This workflow gives you a moment of reflection to ask yourself:

Am I adding valuable content to my PKM or just clutter?

Always consider you'll face these two scenarios:

1. Information that seems life-changing when you capture it might appear irrelevant later when you process it.
2. Information that seems trivial today might become crucial tomorrow due to changing circumstances or insights.

The Process stage involves going through your inbox, analyzing each item, and deciding what to do with it.

You might be wondering when to process each inbox, but for now, don't worry about that. We'll cover it in future chapters when we dive into the Task Management system.

For now, just focus on asking yourself this question for each item in your inbox: Should I do something with this information?

This is where our mental model, The Thought Lab, comes into play.

The Thought Lab helps you determine if the information needs action.

After going through the Discover and Capture stages, you've gained a broader perspective on the information, which is why we recommend waiting a day or two between these stages. This waiting period helps you approach the information more analytically and less emotionally.

In The Thought Lab, ask yourself these questions:

- Does this information enhance my existing knowledge significantly?
- Is it worth diving deeper into?
- Does it impact my current or upcoming projects?
- Are there immediate steps that come to mind?

If you answer YES to any of these questions, move on to the next stage: Action.

If you answer NO to all of them, you have two options:

1. Discard the item if it isn't valuable at all.
2. Store the item in your Shallow Thinking system if you consider it might be useful in the future.

Storing an item in the Shallow Thinking system simply means adding context to it.

Context involves adding relevant (but easy to add) details to the captured item, also known as metadata.

Metadata is "information about information" and helps with understanding and retrieval later on.

Use buckets to provide context to your captured information. These storage areas can be organized by Current Projects, Key Elements, and Topics, as described in The Capturing Beast.

And remember: You can add any piece of content to one or more areas.

After going through the discovering, capturing, and

processing stages, you can be confident that your information is in the right place.

Next, we'll discuss what to do with the items you want to take action on in the next stage of The Knowledge Management Cycle: Action.

2.2.2.5 STAGE 4: ACTION

"Done is better than perfect." — Sheryl Sandberg

T aking action based on information involves two main options.

The first one is pretty straightforward: If the information leads to clear, well-defined steps and you know what needs to be done, jot down those actions. Add them to your Task Management system or, if it affects your team, your Project Management system.

But sometimes, though, information needs more time for consideration. This is where your Deep Thinking system comes into play.

This isn't just about pondering. It's about connecting this new information with what you already have stored in your PKM system.

There are many things you can do:

- Find connections between this new insight and what you already know and have stored.
- Conduct further research.
- Refine or expand your current understanding.
- Introduce a fresh perspective on an ongoing project or topic.

Deep thinking has no limits. It depends on your personal approach, criteria, needs, and goals.

Often, you'll uncover new insights, innovations, or ways to leverage your knowledge through this process.

It might spark a new project idea, a product concept, or a clearer strategic vision.

Being able to shuffle through your stored information, to zoom in and out of concepts and ideas, is crucial.

That's why you should always choose tools that foster deep thinking and resonate with your thinking patterns.

Yet, there's a final and essential stage in The Knowledge Management Cycle.

Once you've synthesized and made sense of the information, it might be time to share it, especially if it could benefit your team or a broader audience, like your entire company or the public.

This is the moment when you proceed to the final phase of The Knowledge Management Cycle: Share.

2.2.2.6 STAGE 5: SHARE

"Sharing knowledge is the most fundamental act of friendship. Because it is a way you can give something without losing something." — Richard Stallman

B efore sharing an idea or thought, please, always ask yourself: Is this truly worth sharing?

Reflect on these questions:

- Does the idea make sense?
- What potential benefits can the business or a broader audience gain from it?

Taking this step is crucial. The goal is to avoid introducing unnecessary confusion or distractions.

Hence, it's essential to spend time on your own evaluating the merit of your idea. Identify any weaknesses, issues, or inconsistencies. Essentially, challenge your idea by trying to kill it!

If it resists the battle, it means it's really worth sharing.

Always remember this: Deep personal reflection should always precede group reflection.

With so many voices and ideas already present in the world, ensure that what you're adding is truly valuable. Your colleagues and the larger community will thank you for it.

At the Paperless Movement®, we developed The Idea Incubator.

This mental model allows us to present ideas, evaluate them as a group, and determine their viability. We will clearly explain it in future chapters inside the Project Management system.

We encourage you to explore it, as we do believe it could revolutionize how your team harnesses collective thought.

The beauty of sharing ideas lies in the feedback and diverse perspectives you receive. This helps test the strength of your concept, uncover overlooked challenges, and even highlight unexpected opportunities.

Collective thought is powerful!

If you've given deep thought to an idea and believe in its potential, don't hesitate to share. It's how businesses and the world evolve, and more importantly, how you also grow personally!

2. 3 STAGE 3: OUTPUT (ACTION)

"Knowledge is not power. Knowledge is only potential power. Action is power." — Tony Robbins

Output is the third stage in ICOR®. It's where you move from information to action, transforming ideas into tasks, projects, and more.

This section will introduce you to multiple concepts and workflows to help you plan, manage, and execute these actions effectively to achieve your goals.

To make your learning easier, we've split this section of the book into two parts using the same criteria as our ICOR® Framework: Personal Project Management (PPM) and Business Project Management (BPM).

This will help you understand how everything fits together.

Personal Project Management or, what's commonly named as Task Management, focuses on tasks that only affect you. Business Project Management covers tasks that impact your team.

By distinguishing between these areas, you'll learn how to organize both yourself and your team efficiently. This approach ensures you can plan, execute, and complete tasks to reach your goals seamlessly.

Taking action is how you progress. It gives you a sense of purpose and achievement as you see things moving forward consistently, just as you planned.

Action turns your thoughts, dreams, and aspirations into tangible realities.

We're excited to explore this with you! Are you ready to dive in?

2.3.1 TASK MANAGEMENT

"You get extraordinary outcomes by doing ordinary things for extraordinary periods of time." — Alex Hormozi

This section will guide you in creating a Task Management system tailored for today's fast-paced and unpredictable business world.

Our goal is to help you establish a reliable system that lets you navigate your days on autopilot, no matter the unexpected challenges you encounter.

This system will be flexible enough to support you consistently, providing peace of mind and ensuring you always perform at your best. It will also ensure you stay on the right path toward your goals, progressing step by step each day. By compounding these daily efforts, you'll achieve your big goals.

We understand the daily grind of a busy professional because we live it ourselves at the Paperless Movement®. In this section, we'll introduce you to the system we use daily. It has helped us reduce anxiety, make the grind easier, and turn busyness into a positive force.

For us, being busy means actively accomplishing tasks without burning out.

Our system, refined over decades, meets all our needs and, more importantly, yours.

You'll learn how to handle any task that comes your way; whether it's a sudden idea, an email from your boss, or a message from a teammate.

You'll know exactly how to capture, plan, execute, and complete it, achieving the ultimate goal of any Task Management system.

We'll start with the essential concepts and then walk you through the key workflows.

You'll learn how to understand, internalize, design, and implement these workflows using the best tools available.

It's time to get things done!

2.3.1.1 CONCEPTS

2.3.1.1.1 PLAN, EXECUTE, COMPLETE: THE TASK MANAGEMENT BLUEPRINT

"Most people overestimate what they can do in one year and underestimate what they can do in ten years." — *Bill Gates*

The first concept you need to grasp is the scope of Task Management within this book.

Task Management refers to the organization, tracking, and completion of work-related tasks that are solely your responsibility.

Importantly, this does not include tasks related to your personal life.

However, you'll find that once you start working using the ICOR® methodology, you'll naturally use it for your personal life and planning as well.

We're focusing on your professional responsibilities; the tasks you need to handle to achieve your business goals, those associated with your company.

Task Management is all about boosting your individual productivity and effectiveness, using strategies to get things done efficiently.

As you will see, Task Management spans one week, with a particular emphasis on daily organization.

2.3.1.1.2 SHALLOW WORK VS. DEEP WORK: THE ART OF BALANCING

"Lost time is never found again." — *Benjamin Franklin*

In today's fast-paced world, understanding Shallow Work and Deep Work can significantly boost your productivity and the quality of your work.

These concepts, introduced by Georgetown University professor Cal Newport in his book *"Deep Work: Rules for Focused Success in a Distracted World,"* highlight different ways we engage with our tasks.

Shallow Work includes tasks that don't require much brainpower and are often done while distracted or with low energy. These tasks, such as responding to emails, handling routine administrative duties, attending unproductive meetings, or browsing the web, don't create much new value and are easy to replicate.

In contrast, Deep Work refers to the ability to focus without distraction on cognitively demanding tasks.

When you're in a state of Deep Work, you're fully immersed in your task, pushing your cognitive abilities to their limit. This type of work generates new value, improves your skills, and is hard to replicate.

Examples of Deep Work include developing a company strategy, designing a new product, writing a sales pitch, preparing a detailed report, structuring a lecture, or learning a new essential skill for your business.

Cultivating a Deep Work practice can lead to massive benefits. It helps you make significant progress towards your big goals by consistently building upon your daily efforts. It enhances your productivity and ensures that the work you do is of the highest quality.

While Deep Work is crucial, it's important to acknowledge that not all Shallow Work can be eliminated. Many Shallow Work tasks are essential for the day-to-day operation of a business.

The key is to effectively balance and manage your time between these two types of work:

1. **Identify and prioritize**. Begin by identifying which tasks are Deep Work and which are Shallow Work. Prioritize your Deep Work tasks to ensure they get the focus they need.
2. **Create a schedule**. Allocate specific blocks of time for Deep Work, ensuring you're working during your peak productive hours. Use the remaining time for Shallow Work.
3. **Minimize distractions**. Set up your work environment to minimize distractions during Deep Work periods. Turn off notifications, close unnecessary tabs, and let others know you're in a focused work mode.
4. **Reflect and adjust**. Regularly reflect on your work habits and adjust your schedule as needed to maintain a healthy balance between Deep Work and Shallow Work.

By understanding and applying the principles of Deep Work and Shallow Work, you'll enhance your productivity and achieve your goals more efficiently.

Make a conscious effort to engage deeply with your most important tasks, and you'll see a marked improvement in both your work quality and personal satisfaction.

2.3.1.1.3 FROM CONFUSION TO CLARITY: TASKS, SPEEDIES, AND REMINDERS EXPLAINED

"It is not that we have a short space of time, but that we waste much of it." — Seneca

T o truly master Task Management, you need to grasp three key concepts: Task, Speedy, and Reminder.

These terms often get mixed up in everyday language, causing confusion.

At the Paperless Movement®, we emphasize the importance of understanding each concept because this understanding ensures we use the correct names consistently, which is crucial for various workflows we will describe later on.

Accurate naming helps us identify items and know what actions to take.

According to ICOR® terminology, the only actionable item in your productivity system is a Task.

We recommend starting the name of a Task with an action verb, such as "Write Report," "Design Logo," or "Prepare Meeting Agenda."

This "verb rule" makes tasks identifiable and encourages action, boosting motivation to complete them.

When a Task becomes complex, break it down into smaller tasks, or subtasks.

In this case, rename the main Task without a verb, as the subtasks become the actionable items starting with a verb.

To make tasks with subtasks stand out in your system as they've now become containers of actionable items, consider naming them in all caps. For example: REPORT, LOGO, MEETING AGENDA.

Now, let's distinguish between two other concepts: Speedy and

Reminder.

In ICOR® terms, a Task typically takes 15 minutes to 3 hours to complete. If it takes longer, we highly recommend splitting it into multiple tasks. This strategy is essential for effective day and week planning as you will see in future chapters.

A Speedy is a shorter task, one you can complete in less than 15 minutes.

Tasks need planning and should be scheduled based on criteria like due date, estimated time, or required energy level. They usually demand Deep Work, focus and concentration.

Speedies, however, require minimal planning. Just decide on the date they should be done, as they involve Shallow Work.

Finally, let's understand Reminders.

A Reminder is created when a Task or Speedy needs to be executed on a specific date and time. It acts as an alarm to alert you that an item needs attention.

It's crucial not to confuse Speedies or Tasks with Reminders. Speedies and Tasks are actions to execute, while Reminders are alarms to jog your memory.

Reminders can also be used for other items in your productivity system, like for example, events.

2.3.1.1.4 BEYOND THE OVERLAP: UNDERSTANDING TIME MANAGEMENT AND TASK MANAGEMENT

"Time feels abstract and that makes it hard to be intentional with it." — Alexander Cunningham

A t the Paperless Movement®, we've observed that many people confuse two crucial concepts: Time Management and Task Management.

It's an easy mix-up because these concepts do overlap.

However, understanding the difference is key to designing effective workflows and choosing the right tools.

If you're not clear on the concepts, you might end up with tools that don't help, leading to chaos in your productivity system.

In the world of productivity, Time Management means organizing and planning your time across various activities, not just tasks because, as a busy professional, your time is also spent on meetings, commutes, and other events.

Time Management is about managing all these activities, focusing on the time itself, not just what you're doing, and here's a breakdown of all it involves:

- **Prioritization**. Determine which tasks are most important and allocate your time and energy accordingly. It's about putting the most critical items at the top of your task list.
- **Self-awareness**. Know when you work best. Are you a morning person, or do you hit your stride in the afternoon? Understanding your productivity peaks helps you work smarter.
- **Planning**. Using our ICOR® methodology, we've developed a mental model called PEA (you'll see it in future chapters) to manage tasks efficiently and align them with your goals. PEA stands for Plan, Execute, Align. Time blocking is a key aspect, where you set

specific chunks of time for different tasks or events.

- **Delegation**. If a task can be done by someone else, delegate it. This frees up your time for tasks that require your expertise.
- **Avoiding procrastination**. Find strategies to stop putting things off and start tackling tasks on time.
- **Setting boundaries**. Learn to say no to tasks that aren't important or don't help you reach your goals. Focus on what truly matters. Save time.
- **Continuous review and adjustment**. Regularly review how you're spending your time and adjust your approach to become more efficient. It's like doing a self-audit to keep improving.

In short, Time Management is about knowing what to do, when to do it, and how to do it efficiently while being ready to adjust your plan as needed.

Planners are the best tools for scheduling and timing, as they are specifically designed for that purpose.

Task Management is about defining, organizing, prioritizing, and managing tasks effectively to meet your goals.

It overlaps with Time Management in terms of organizing and prioritizing but focuses solely on the task itself, almost like looking at a snapshot without considering time-related aspects.

Here's what Task Management involves:

- **Task identification**. Understand how each task fits into the bigger picture. Ask questions like: Which project does this task belong to? or What goals are connected to this task?
- **Task analysis**. Break down each task into smaller, manageable parts. This makes it easier to tackle them one by one.

- **Resource allocation**. Determine what you need for each task, whether it's information, tools, or assigning someone responsible for it.

By focusing solely on the task, Task Management is about setting up tasks in a way that makes your work smoother, less stressful, and more efficient. This helps you use your resources wisely and achieve your goals more effectively.

Tools like Task Management software, to-do lists, and project management tools are designed specifically for this purpose.

Implementing Task Management and Time Management with the right tools becomes straightforward once you understand the concepts:

- **Individual Tasks**. Use tools like Things or Todoist.
- **Team Tasks**. Use Project Management tools like ClickUp, Linear, or Asana for coordinating and tracking group progress.
- **Time Management**. Use planners such as Sunsama or Akiflow to schedule and manage time, combining both tasks and events.

Task managers often include time-related features like start and due dates, which can cause confusion. People may focus on planning and execution, leading to overlapping.

View these time features as preliminary steps for planning. They provide an initial framework, which you carry into your planner, where genuine Time Management should happen.

Regular reviews of task status and overall progress are crucial for monitoring and adjusting strategies and plans.

Planners introduce reality into your schedule by imposing necessary limits, helping you prioritize and make decisions. They shift focus from endless possibilities to a world of restrictions and limitations (time), essential for bringing your plans to life.

2.3.1.1.5 CONSTRAINTS AND FREEDOM: CALENDARS VS. PLANNERS

"Your to-do list is the ideal Sunday evening theory. Your calendar is the brutal Monday to Friday practice." — *Shreyas Doshi*

O nce you understand the difference between Time Management and Task Management, it's important to dive a little bit deeper into Time Management.

This will help you get the most out of essential tools like calendars and planners. Although they might seem similar, as you will see, they are quite different.

We always state every tool is designed with a specific purpose in mind, something it excels at. This main feature is the tool's strength, while other functions might just be additional, less effective features.

Many software companies claim their tools can handle a wide range of tasks in various scenarios.

However, this is not always the most efficient approach.

Using a tool beyond its primary purpose can lead to complications. You might find yourself creating workarounds or using the tool in ways it wasn't designed for, which can disrupt your workflow and the way you think and work. Over time, this can turn a smooth workflow into a challenging one.

Then, you might start searching for alternative tools that better suit specific tasks and operations you're struggling with. This can lead to a fragmented productivity system where you're unsure where to store or manage your information and actions, causing stress and confusion.

A common example of this issue is with calendars and planners.

A calendar is a way to organize and keep track of time,

usually broken down into days, weeks, months, and years.

While originally calendars were just for scheduling events or appointments, recent advances in software productivity tools have expanded their use.

Now, you can use calendars to set tasks, deadlines, plan out project timelines, and manage various other kinds of information and activities.

On the other hand, we have planners, which are tools designed for Time Management.

Time Management, as we saw in the previous chapter, involves organizing and dividing your time among various activities.

However, a problem arises here. People often get confused about which tool to use for managing everything: events, appointments, tasks, and more.

This confusion is compounded by a technique known as Time Blocking.

Time Blocking is a method of Time Management where you divide your day into specific periods, each dedicated to a certain task or activity. Instead of tackling tasks randomly, you assign a specific time slot to each task, reducing the chances of procrastination and distractions.

This brings up several questions:

- Where should you keep track of your tasks?
- Where do you organize your meetings?
- How can you effectively use the Time Blocking technique?

Understanding the distinction and purpose of these concepts is key to managing your time and tasks efficiently.

There are three basic concepts you need to know:

1. Constraints vs. Freedom.

Constraints often suggest being limited or restricted.

While many believe constraints limit freedom, they actually help navigate complex scenarios, especially in the busy life of a professional.

Constraints clarify what needs to be done and the steps you need to follow.

Freedom implies the lack of restrictions, allowing one to act as they wish. It represents the idea of being unbound.

2. Purpose of a Calendar.

A calendar is a tool to record constraints; the unavoidable commitments like events, meetings, or appointments. These are essential and missing them is not an option.

For managing these constraints, tools like Google Calendar, iCal, or Outlook are ideal, as they are specifically designed to keep track of such commitments.

3. Role of Planners.

Planners are designed to help manage your time.

They allow you to organize all time-consuming activities, including tasks.

Tasks represent freedom as you decide when to complete them based on various criteria.

Planners are suited for the Time Blocking technique, with examples like Akiflow or Sunsama.

Don't get confused because planners use calendar views to show you the information. That doesn't mean they're calendars at all!

Planners should be used to include all events from your

calendar tool and all the tasks you want to plan coming from your Task Management and Project Management tools. This helps manage time effectively.

When planning, prioritize tasks around the constraints (events from your calendar) and allocate time for them.

This approach ensures maximum productivity with minimal effort.

❖ ❖ ❖

By using calendars specifically for time-sensitive items like events, meetings, or appointments, you totally remove the need for decision-making whenever these items come up.

Calendar tools are designed to efficiently capture and manage them for you.

Having immediate access to all your events on a calendar tool is incredibly helpful for daily planning. You can easily see the time slots already blocked by mandatory items like meetings or appointments. This visibility allows you to strategically schedule your tasks around these fixed commitments.

Another useful strategy is to set goals for completing certain tasks either before an event begins or in the gaps between events. This approach helps in prioritizing and managing tasks more effectively, avoiding the pitfalls of Parkinson's Law, which states that work expands to fill the time available for its completion.

Choosing the right tools for specific tasks and workflows is crucial for building an effective productivity system.

Always remember this: planners are tools designed to manage your time. While you can choose when to execute your tasks, you don't have the same flexibility with scheduled events. Therefore, using these tools wisely can greatly enhance your productivity system.

By following these guidelines, you can create a clear, efficient workflow that allows you to stay organized and focused. Embrace the primary purposes of your tools, and you'll find that your productivity will soar.

2.3.1.1.6 FROM ANXIETY TO CONTROL: REDEFINING WHAT PLANNING REALLY MEANS

"Don't let what you cannot do interfere with what you can do." —John Wooden

Many busy professionals feel anxious when they can't accomplish all their planned tasks. This mindset, however, reflects a misguided approach to planning and its underlying concept.

Planning isn't about meticulously scheduling every single task. Instead, it should serve as a theoretical roadmap for what you'd like to achieve.

When planning your week, just focus on two main goals:

1. **Create a structured plan that makes sense to you**. This gives you a sense of control, security, and calm.
2. **Facilitate easy comparison between planned tasks and unexpected events that can pop up at any moment**. This way, you only need to compare one planned task with one unexpected one, making it easier to manage changes.

Think of planning as a technique to ensure you're always working on the most relevant tasks based on your priorities, time, and, most importantly, your current circumstances.

Considering your circumstances is what makes our Task Management system so powerful. It's designed to be fully flexible and adaptable, reflecting the dynamic and ever-changing nature of today's world.

2.3.1.1.7 ACHIEVE MORE: THE MAGIC OF WEEKLY GOALS AND THE HIGHLIGHT OF THE DAY

"It's impossible to fail when you do your best every day."
— Team Paperless Movement®

T here are two key concepts that can supercharge your Task Management system: Weekly Goals and Highlight of the Day.

These concepts encourage consistent daily action and help you accomplish your tasks and, consequently your goals, efficiently.

Weekly Goals are the tasks you aim to complete within the week.

It's important not to confuse these tasks with the larger, more significant goals you define in a Project Management system, elements we'll describe in future chapters.

Weekly Goals are more immediate and manageable, that's why they're tasks linked to any goal in your productivity system.

Highlight of the Day is a single, specific weekly goal you commit to accomplishing each day. Just one!

By focusing on just one Highlight each day, you ensure that task gets done without any excuses.

By incorporating these two concepts, your Task Management system will guide you effortlessly, telling you what needs to be done rather than the other way around. This is where real productivity happens.

To summarize:

- **Weekly Goals** are the tasks you plan to finish this week.
- **Highlight of the Day** is the most important task you choose to complete today, ensuring consistent progress.

By sticking to these two concepts, you'll find that achieving your goals is just a matter of time.

2.3.1.1.8 ROUTINES: THE CORNERSTONE OF YOUR PRODUCTIVITY SYSTEM

"We are what we repeatedly do. Excellence, then, is not an act, but a habit." — Aristotle

At this point, we're about to make one of the boldest statements in this book. So, please, pay attention: Routines are the most essential concept you need to understand, master, and implement to turn anything into a system.

Think of Routines as the foundation of your productivity system and the way you should work from now on.

This is the moment when the physical and digital parts of your brain truly merge into one, unified by this life-changing concept.

Routines are the essential building blocks that ensure your productivity system operates smoothly and effectively.

Without Routines, your so-called "productivity system" isn't really a system at all.

This is a common scenario for the busy professionals who seek help from the Paperless Movement®.

Many lack a productivity system simply because they don't understand what a system truly is.

Here's what you need to grasp: Systems are the workflows that lead you to achieve your goals, the results you want, and the outcomes you aim to deliver.

Once you implement a system, you can be 100% confident that your goals will be met. It all starts with setting up the system and then letting it run its course. It's just a matter of time before you reach the destination you've set.

Routines become the main components to start building a reliable productivity system. A well-designed productivity system that'll guide you, at any moment, on the steps you should take to reach your goals.

And, we should never forget that this is the ultimate purpose.

2.3.1.1.9 FINDING HARMONY: INTEGRATE BALANCE INTO YOUR BUSY LIFE

"Balance is not something you find, it's something you create." —Jana Kingsford

Maintaining balance in life is essential. It positions you to perform at your best without falling into anxiety, stress, or burnout.

That's why it's crucial to integrate the concept of Balance into your daily and weekly routines consistently.

Your Task Management system should be your tool to achieve this Balance.

Each day, ask yourself how you envision your day unfolding. And please, be honest with yourself. In reality, you can handle no more than 7-10 tasks a day, including both major tasks and speedies.

Unexpected events will arise: urgent tasks, annoying calls, unplanned meetings, unforeseen events, and other challenges familiar to any busy professional.

To ensure you meet your Weekly Goals, allocate 4-6 hours for planned work each day, and reserve 2-4 hours as "buffer time."

This buffer helps you manage unexpected situations and account for any underestimations in task duration, especially when you're new to this approach.

Remember, we humans often overestimate what we can achieve in a day or week but underestimate what we can accomplish in a month, quarter, or year.

That's why we at the Paperless Movement® believe in long-term planning. We know what can be achieved over extended periods if we consistently meet our short-term goals each day and week.

Eventually, your efforts will compound, leading to amazing

results.

Returning to our main point, when you limit your planned daily work to 4-6 hours, you'll realize you can't do everything. You'll need to make sacrifices, but they are not truly sacrifices. They just reflect reality.

Once you've adjusted your plans from dream to reality, ensure everything is balanced within your week.

Then, each day, repeat the process: evaluate if your day aligns with your goals, if your morning and afternoon have a balanced number of tasks, and if the tasks suit your energy levels and circumstances.

2.3.1.1.10 FOCUS AND FLEXIBILITY: THE DUAL STRENGTHS OF TIME BLOCKING

"If you don't separate yourself from distractions, your distractions will separate you from your goals." — Steve Harvey

Time Blocking is a powerful Time Management technique where you divide your day into dedicated blocks of time.

Each block is reserved for a specific task or group of tasks, allowing (and forcing) you to focus exclusively on one thing at a time.

The beauty of this technique is that it naturally helps you build a routine-based system (our ultimate goal), as many of the blocks will align with your daily habits, creating a structured yet flexible schedule.

But, we've detected that many busy professionals misunderstand what Time Blocking truly means.

The goal isn't to create a flawless, perfectly scheduled calendar from 9 to 10, 10 to 11, and so on. Such a rigid approach can fall apart the moment a task takes longer than expected or any unexpected event pops up, leading to constant reorganization and more time spent planning than doing.

Always remember this: Achieving your goals comes from action, not over-organization.

Time Blocking should be a quick and straightforward way to know what to focus on at any given moment.

It should be adaptable, flexible, and ready to accommodate unexpected events throughout your day.

The essence of Time Blocking is creating sequential blocks that guide your tasks. While you can use specific times as references, you can also use blocks as those references. For example, complete tasks A and B before moving on to task C, which might be a scheduled meeting.

This technique visually illustrates the constraints of time, emphasizing that while task lists are endless, time is finite.

The goal is to have a reference point to ensure your plan aligns with your current situation at any moment.

If not, you can quickly rearrange your blocks, postponing or even canceling tasks that no longer make sense. This flexibility forces you to prioritize effectively.

We believe that Time Blocking pushes you to prioritize effectively, keeping you focused on your most important tasks: your Weekly Goals.

We highly recommend assigning one of your Weekly Goals to each day and to specific blocks. This way, you'll achieve at least five goals by the end of the week, ensuring your attention remains on what truly matters.

Trust us, this approach is all you need to make significant progress towards any goal, no matter how ambitious it may be.

Give Time Blocking a try, and you'll be amazed at how it boosts your productivity!

2.3.1.1.11 THE SEQUENTIAL MIND: EMBRACING OUR NATURAL WORKFLOW

"The true price of anything you do is the amount of time you exchange for it." — Henry David Thoreau

I n the previous chapter, we discussed how one of the most significant benefits of Time Blocking is achieving Sequentiality.

Sequentiality is so crucial that any effective Task Management system should naturally encourage it. But why is it so essential?

Because it taps into our core nature as human beings.

We are fundamentally sequential creatures. Yes, that's what we are. And yes, that's what you are.

Understanding this concept is crucial because it will bring clarity to how you design and implement your productivity system.

Your brain isn't built to handle multiple cognitively demanding tasks simultaneously. Multitasking goes against your natural tendencies, leading to stress, mistakes, and reduced productivity.

It's always more effective to focus on one task at a time, execute it well, and then move on to the next.

The Task Management system, we will help you create, will foster sequentiality at every step, making it second nature through consistent practice.

You'll find yourself naturally adopting this "one task at a time" approach because it promotes:

- **Focus**. By avoiding distractions and concentrating on a single task, you free yourself from worrying about anything else.
- **Accomplishment**. The likelihood of achieving your

goals increases because, once you start something, you push yourself to complete it, as there's no other option. This ensures tasks get done and, as a result, your goals are accomplished.

- **Prioritization**. You focus on only one task at a time. That's the golden rule. You have no choice but to prioritize between task A and task B. It's simple, quick, manageable, and effective.

2.3.1.1.12 REIMAGINING TASK MANAGEMENT: LEVERAGING MULTIPLE TOOLS FOR MAXIMUM EFFICIENCY

"Divide et impera." (Divide and Conquer) — Julius Caesar

L et's wrap up our discussion on Task Management concepts with one that can truly revolutionize your productivity mindset and how you approach the design and build of your Task Management system.

This idea is a game-changer, and we encourage you to embrace it. It will enhance not just your Task Management system, but your entire productivity system, ultimately improving your work and outcomes.

Today, many software tools that weren't originally designed for Task Management are now incorporating Task Management features. This presents a great opportunity for you to leverage these tools to your advantage. Don't let it slip by!

Yet, many "productivity gurus" recommend always sending every task to a single, dedicated, one-and-only Task Management tool.

However, we respectfully disagree, based on decades of extensive experimentation testing hundreds of techniques, including this "one-tool" approach. Our findings are straightforward: The less cluttered your tools, the better your performance.

While it's commonly believed that consolidating everything into one tool can boost productivity, offer control, and provide a clear overview, this approach only works if you're not dealing with hundreds or thousands of tasks daily. This is often the case with a Task Management system that busy professionals rely on every day.

Our recommendation is to make the most of the Task

Management features these non-Task Management tools bring to the table. This approach leads to a critical productivity goal: clarity.

Clarity is key to performing at your best and maintaining high productivity levels.

When we talk about non-Task Management tools, we mean software like Slack (a team communication tool), Superhuman (an email client), Readwise Read-Later (a read-later tool), and many others you likely use every day.

At the Paperless Movement®, we use even more of these non-Task Management tools within our Task Management system.

Imagine the chaos of funneling every task from these tools into one main, one-and-only Task Management tool. It would quickly become overloaded and unmanageable, leading to a productivity breakdown.

A cluttered system equals inaction and unproductivity; a nightmare for any busy professional. A lack of clarity always leads to chaos and unproductiveness.

In this book, we'll introduce you to simple workflows that keep your Task Management system clean and efficient.

Even with millions of tasks, you'll feel in control and productive, trusting a system you can endlessly leverage.

2.3.1.2 WORKFLOWS

"Never let a short-term desire get in the way of a long-term goal." — Curtis Martin

In this chapter, you'll discover that mastering just five workflows can help you navigate your weeks and days smoothly and efficiently. These workflows are designed to eliminate friction and make your daily life more manageable.

That's right, only five workflows, not thirty or more!

We've distilled the essentials to help busy professionals handle their schedules with coherence, control, and, most importantly, satisfaction. By achieving tangible results day after day, you'll experience a sense of accomplishment without missing a beat.

Each workflow has been carefully crafted to ensure that implementation feels natural. You can easily integrate them into your current tools or any others you prefer.

Here's a glimpse of what we'll cover in the upcoming chapters:

- **Weekly planning**. Learn how to plan your week effectively, ensuring you stay on top of your tasks and relentlessly move toward your goals.
- **Weekly review**. Discover a simple method to review your week in just 15-30 minutes, helping you stay on track without any excuses.
- **Daily planning**. Understand how to start each day with a clear plan that you know you'll accomplish.
- **Daily routines**. Uncover the key elements to build a real Task Management system.
- **Managing Speedies**. Find out how to handle Speedies efficiently, maintaining your momentum without feeling overwhelmed by their volume.

Get ready to transform your productivity with these

straightforward and powerful workflows!

2.3.1.2.1 WEEKLY PLANNING MADE EASY: STEPS TO A STRESS-FREE WEEK

"Plans are nothing; planning is everything." — Dwight D. Eisenhower

L et's start by clearly stating our ultimate goal for this workflow: Ensuring your week is perfectly organized, so you know exactly what to do and when to do it.

This workflow has five sequential steps you just need to follow:

1. Brain Zen.
2. Goal Alignment.
3. Schedule.
4. Balance.
5. Re-balance.

Let's take a closer look at each of them in detail.

The goal of the Brain Zen is to achieve complete peace of mind by thoroughly reviewing all your tasks and systems, ensuring nothing is overlooked and everything is noted down.

This includes going through both your Project Management and Task Management systems.

Here's how to do it.

Open your Project Management system and check:

1. Tasks planned for this week.
2. Tasks that don't have a day assigned and should be done this week.
3. Tasks originally planned for other weeks that need to be done this week due to changes in your plans, thoughts, or circumstances.
4. Overdue tasks that should be done this week.

At the end of this process, you should have a clear list of all the tasks, coming from your Project Management system, that you aim to complete or, at least, dedicate your time this week.

The process you need to follow in your Task Management system is exactly the same so you end up with the same result: tasks you aim to complete or dedicate your time this week.

It's important that, in this process, you include your Speedies, as they need to be planned too.

By the end of the Brain Zen process, you should be 100% sure everything that needs to be done this week is perfectly listed.

That's how you achieve peace of mind, calm, and control as you're sure nothing will fall through the cracks.

Now, it's the moment to move to step 2, to ensure alignment between your tasks and the goals you or your team have previously set.

Obviously, from all the tasks you've selected for this week, not all of them will be linked to your goals, no matter if they belong to your team or just yourself, as many are simple Speedies you need to execute and some others are operational tasks you need to complete to keep your business and life running.

That's why by literally marking the tasks that are fully aligned to your goals, you are able to make them shine, to be differentiated from the rest. That's how you start "creating signal and removing noise."

We call those aligned tasks Weekly Goals, and we recommend two things:

1. **Don't be too ambitious**. Just choose the five most crucial goals and leave the rest for the next week. Once you're used to this workflow, you can gradually increase that number. For now, start simple. It's much better to consistently accomplish five Weekly Goals than to aim for more and risk underperforming, potentially achieving even less than five.

2. **Try to mark them in your tool using any of the features most Task Management tools have: a star, a flag, a special icon, an emoji…** The goal of this tactic is to clearly identify those Weekly Goals at any moment, at a glance, especially when you're "in the middle of the storm."

Now that you have all your tasks of the week and your Weekly Goals perfectly identified, it's the moment to move to step three: Schedule.

This step's goal is quite straightforward: to ensure every task is assigned (scheduled) to a specific day.

The moment you hear or see the word Schedule, you need to think about Time Management.

At this point, you're shifting from "what to do" (Brain Zen and Goal Alignment) to "when to do it." This means you're now focusing on your most precious asset: your time.

This is the moment we highly recommend using a planner, as we consider planners the best tools possible to manage time.

These types of tools are so great because they allow you to merge all your time-consuming items, no matter if they're events or tasks coming from any of your action systems (your Project Management system, your Task Management system, or your calendar).

A planner also helps you run and schedule your routines, a key component of any productivity system, and one of the essential and crucial time-consumers of any Task Management system.

You need to schedule each task on a specific day.

Start by assigning each of your five Weekly Goals to a specific day of the week. This way, you'll complete at least five goals by the end of the week, giving you a motivational boost!

Then, schedule the rest of tasks on the day you believe it would be best executed.

At this moment you don't need to worry about the exact time for each task, as that'll be covered in the Daily Planning workflow we'll explain later on.

Once finished, your entire week should be planned. However, beware: this is still theoretical.

You need to move it to "real life," which is what you'll do in the next step: Balance.

This fourth stage is based on the concept Balance we've previously explained. It suggests that you should block 4-6 hours for planned work and 2-4 hours as "buffer time."

That "planned work" should include two main items:

1. Your Weekly Goals.
2. Your Routines.

Your Weekly Goals guarantee alignment, the only way to be sure what you're doing today will contribute to accomplish your goals in the future.

Your Routines guarantee you never stop doing the things you should constantly do to keep your business and life running.

Routines allow you to run things on autopilot, the best way possible to reduce the energy you consume and the time you dedicate to the things.

The "buffer time" ensures you're covered no matter what unexpected event appears, or if you underestimate the time required for any task.

As it usually happens, we're pretty sure the moment you check all your scheduled tasks in this Balance stage, you've moved far beyond those 4-6 hours for planned work.

If this is the case, you have no choice: postpone the less important tasks to the next week.

Don't worry about this. In fact, feel happy, as your Task Management system is telling you the truth, the reality of your work life.

Once this is done, it's time to move on to the fifth and final step of your Weekly Planning: Re-balance.

Rebalancing is nothing else but checking again how your Weekly Planning looks like.

It's a quick process, a final assessment, where you can ask yourself these types of questions:

- Does each day's plan make sense?
- Have I planned at least one Weekly Goal each day?
- Am I sure I haven't scheduled more than 4-6 planned hours each day?

By the end of this process, you should feel at ease, confident that everything makes sense and is achievable.

Don't worry if this workflow seems slow or overwhelming right now. We've explained it in detail to help you understand all the "baby steps" you need to follow. Once you grasp the overall idea, you'll execute it quickly, smoothly moving from one stage to the next, and even overlapping some of them.

Remember, your brain works incredibly fast. It just needs clarity on what you're asking it to do. By internalizing this workflow and making it second nature, you'll achieve that clarity (and your brain too).

For example, at the Paperless Movement®, we execute this workflow in just 15 minutes or even less.

This happens not just because we've executed it for decades, but due to a crucial aspect: the moment you have a perfect productivity system running, the need to organize and put things into order disappears, as it's just by running the system that those things happen on their own.

We explain this in our next workflow: Weekly Review.

2.3.1.2.2 TRANSFORM YOUR REVIEWS: THE SEAMLESS SYSTEM APPROACH

"To achieve great things, two things are needed: a plan and not quite enough time." — Leonard Bernstein

T his is where you see the true power of the system approach.

Most of the busy professionals who come to the Paperless Movement® tell us they spend hours doing reviews.

For us, reviews never made much sense. We've always aimed for a system that, with just a glance, shows us the whole picture and… the deepest one, if necessary.

We understand that in your hectic life, reviews often get overlooked or forgotten amidst all the things you need to manage. Let's be honest: reviews can be a real pain.

That's why we believe lengthy reviews are a thing of the past. Reviews should be quick and effortless, to the point where you almost don't need to do them at all.

For us at the Paperless Movement®, a Weekly Review takes just a few minutes. Our quarterly reviews, where we define our goals and projects for the entire quarter, take about 2 to 3 hours because everything is crystal clear.

Our productivity system gives us real-time updates, showing us what's happening, where to focus, and how we're performing. Since the system is always up to date, thanks to our constant interactions with it, "old and formal reviews" become almost unnecessary.

If you interact correctly with your productivity system each time, everything stays up to date, eliminating the need for extensive reviews.

Traditional methods often require reviews because things get outdated, and you spend time organizing and reorganizing.

Our approach keeps everything organized at all times.

So, what does a Weekly Review look like in your Task Management system?

It's simple: execute your Weekly Planning.

If your Task Management system is set up correctly, this should only take minutes, not hours.

To make your Weekly Review run smoothly, keep your tasks up to date with planned execution dates.

If you want to use the Weekly Review time to do simple tasks like cleaning up your desktop, go ahead.

Doing these tasks weekly ensures everything stays perfect.

As you can see, this systematic approach is the easiest and most efficient way to stay on top of everything effortlessly.

2.3.1.2.3 DAILY PLANNING: YOUR GUIDE TO DAILY SUCCESS

"Intentional days create a life on purpose." — Adrienne Enns

Now that your week is clearly outlined thanks to your Weekly Planning, it's time to shift your focus to daily execution.

This is a crucial moment because if you get your week and each day under control, you'll start to feel and see yourself at your most productive.

This daily approach works because you're setting aside concerns about yesterday, tomorrow, or the day after, and focusing entirely on today's tasks; the ones you planned in your Weekly Planning.

The approach to Daily Planning is similar to our Weekly Planning at the Paperless Movement®. We always keep our workflows consistent, making them second nature because they're simple and just a few.

By sticking to similar workflows and following the same logical steps, execution becomes a breeze.

For successful Daily Planning, remember the concept of Sequentiality, which we discussed earlier as your ultimate goal for Daily Planning is to define the execution order of each task, avoiding multitasking.

Planners should be your go-to tool for implementing Sequentiality in your work and life.

Here are the five steps for effective Daily Planning:

1. Review your tasks.
2. Assess feasibility.
3. Identify the Highlight of the Day.
4. Order your tasks.

5. Commit and execute.

Let's check them one by one.

Start by reviewing the list of tasks you've planned for today in your Task Management and Project Management systems.

Then, as a second step, ensure your list of tasks for today is still feasible. Things may have changed since you did your Weekly Planning:

- New tasks may have emerged.
- You might have been overly optimistic and planned more tasks than you can complete.
- Priorities may have shifted.
- You might not feel up to certain tasks today due to your mood or circumstances.

Life is unpredictable, especially for a busy professional like you!

The beauty of our Task Management system is its flexibility. It can adapt to your situation at any stage, whether during planning or as your day progresses.

If your task list feels overwhelming, reorganize as you did during your Weekly Planning. Move tasks you can't tackle today to tomorrow or another future date. Trust your system, as it's your reliable partner.

Review and check your list again to ensure you can manage everything listed before moving to the third step: identifying the Highlight of the Day.

The Highlight of the Day is the task essential to progressing towards your goals. It should be one of your Weekly Goals.

This is where your planner comes into play, making things easy by encouraging and guiding you to stay sequential.

Place your Highlight of the Day at the top and enter the

fourth step, by arranging the rest of your tasks based on their execution order below your Highlight of the Day.

To make the arrangement process faster and easier, you can differentiate between tasks for the morning (when your energy is highest) and those for the afternoon (when your energy may dip).

Once you've separated morning and afternoon tasks, defining their sequential order becomes even simpler.

By the end of this process, you should have an ordered list of tasks. Focus only on the task at the top and move to the last and final step: Execution.

This is the moment where you execute the task, complete it, and move on to the next.

But, what happens if an unexpected event appears on your way?

Easy. Compare it with your current task, the one you're working on, and decide which is more important.

Making a choice between two options is straightforward. Our monkey mind is prepared for that!

This is how you ensure you're always doing what matters most. This is real (and easy) prioritization.

Now, with your day planned and a clear order of execution, it's crucial to keep your system updated throughout the whole day.

To make this possible, you need to establish routines, which is our next workflow.

2.3.1.2.4 ROUTINE MASTERY: THE BACKBONE OF AN UNSTOPPABLE PRODUCTIVITY SYSTEM

"You'll never change your life until you change something you do daily. The secret of your success is found in your daily routine." — John C. Maxwell

Your daily Routines are the foundation of your productivity system. They help you design, build, and ultimately run your day smoothly.

By structuring your day around these daily Routines, you shift from "reaction mode" to "proactive mode." This transition creates a positive feedback loop that offers multiple benefits, as it's practical, logical, nice, and friendly.

Daily Routines help you perform at your best, no matter the circumstances. They act as a crucial defense against distractions from the Outer World, giving you a sense of control and security that's essential for true productivity.

To build an effective and robust productivity system, you need to define, create and implement standard workflows. Among the most essential of these are your daily Routines, which you should follow on autopilot.

A daily Routine is essentially a checklist of tasks performed sequentially, simplifying your life and conserving mental energy. Everything is prearranged, so you don't have to decide what to do next.

But that's not the only aspect of daily Routines you need to consider. It's not just about what you do (each task of the checklist); it's also about when you do it. To truly build your productivity system, you need to internalize this second part.

The key is defining when you'll execute each daily Routine.

It's the combination of the content of your daily Routines (the checklist of tasks they contain) and the timing of each daily Routine that enables you to create an effective productivity system.

This is so crucial for you to understand because this is what removes the need to think about "the when" and "the what." You'll have well-defined time slots for each daily Routine, so you'll always know what to do and in what order.

That's how you run your system on autopilot. You do nothing. You don't have to decide anything. Your productivity system simply guides you.

It also ensures that nothing falls through the cracks. You never forget anything because it's all accounted for. You have complete control. You're powerful. You're productive.

This way, you don't waste any unnecessary energy. You save your energy for what truly matters: executing.

You just need to dedicate time to setting up your daily Routines, clearly defining their tasks, execution order, and when you'll perform them. Once that's done, simply refine them whenever you need to add an item. Period.

We recommend establishing at least three daily routines: morning, afternoon, and end-of-day. Here are some examples to inspire you.

Your morning routine might include:

- **Planning your day**, if you haven't already done so the previous evening (which we highly recommend).
- **Checking your inboxes**, such as those in communication, Project Management, Task Management, or Email Management tools.

During your afternoon routine, you might check your inboxes again. This ensures everything is running smoothly: responding to people, delegating tasks, and so on.

By doing this, you're making sure things keep moving in parallel. While you're focused on your tasks, others are completing work on your behalf.

That's why delegating as soon as possible is so crucial.

Finally, you might dedicate your end-of-day routine to two additional tasks:

- **Journaling**, which is great for daily reflection and allows you to pause and savor the satisfaction of successfully completing another day.
- **Planning the next day**. As mentioned before, when you "plan tomorrow today," you can start your day without having to think about what needs to be done. You simply begin executing what's already planned!

Daily Routines consume time and are allocated as time blocks in your planner.

They are essential because they keep your system running smoothly and are the best way to build a comprehensive productivity system end to end.

Since daily Routines take up part of your day, we also recommend only blocking 2-3 hours a day for your Deep Work.

Be honest with yourself. It's difficult to do more than that. When you push Deep Work beyond 3 hours, your performance declines, and you'll end up exhausted in the middle of the day.

If you tally up everything that needs to be done, you'll find that 2-3 hours of Deep Work is enough.

Remember, people tend to overestimate what they can do in a day but underestimate what they can achieve in a month, a quarter, or a year through consistency.

We emphasize: 2-3 hours of Deep Work each day makes a big difference!

And it's not just us who say this. Cal Newport, a prominent figure in the field of Deep Work, asserts:

"Two to three hours of uninterrupted, focused Deep Work can produce higher quality output and greater progress than an entire day filled with distracted, Shallow Work."

By adding these daily Routines to your planner, you can clearly see the constraints of time.

As a result, scheduling other tasks becomes easier because you will always have these standard time blocks each day:

- Deep Work.
- Daily Routines.
- Shallow Work.
- Unexpected events or delays due to underestimation.

You have the flexibility to schedule your daily Routines whenever it suits you, although we always recommend starting your day with Deep Work to make the most of your energy levels.

This ensures that, no matter what happens throughout the day, your Deep Work time block is always covered.

This fosters consistency, which is the key element in progressing towards your goals and achieving success.

2.3.1.2.5 BATCHING SPEEDIES: THE KEY TO STREAMLINE YOUR TASK MANAGEMENT SYSTEM

"Focus on being productive instead of busy." — Tim Ferriss

We've previously distinguished between two concepts: Speedies and Tasks.

Here, we'll go deeper because understanding the differences between them is crucial for several reasons:

- **Prevents clutter**. It keeps your Task Management system clear and focused.
- **Encourages batching**. Batching, as discussed, is a highly effective technique for peak performance.
- **Avoids overwhelm**. It ensures you're not overwhelmed by "trivial tasks," the Speedies, which can disrupt your day.
- **Ensures completion**. It ensures that Speedies are managed and completed because, even though they might seem insignificant due to their short duration, they're still crucial and need your attention. If they weren't important, they wouldn't even exist.

To manage your Speedies effectively, you need to clearly define three stages:

1. **Capture**. Record them in your Single Source of Truth.
2. **Plan**. Determine when you'll execute the Speedy.
3. **Execute**. Complete the Speedy.

Let's check them out one by one.

The moment a new task arises, immediately ask yourself: Is this a Speedy?

If the new task is not a Speedy but a Task because it will take you more than 15 minutes to complete, you should record it in either your Task Management or Project Management tool.

To decide which tool to use, consider the task's impact: if it affects your team, use your Project Management tool; if it only affects you, use your Task Management tool.

However, try to use your Project Management tool as much as possible, because tasks that initially seem personal often end up influencing and having a deep impact in your entire team over time.

If the new task is a Speedy, you can capture and plan it simultaneously because they're so simple.

If a Speedy needs to be done at a specific time, you can set a reminder, so your tool will notify you when it's time to execute and complete it.

Your Single Source of Truth for Speedies could be a specific tool just for Speedies, or you can use a tag to easily identify them in your Task Management or Project Management tool.

After storing and planning your Speedy, you'll get a dopamine boost and your brain can relax, allowing you to focus on what really matters: achieving peak performance.

Now, the question is: When do you execute those Speedies?

That's where daily Routines come into play because if you let Speedies dictate your day, you'll face constant interruptions.

We recommend tackling Speedies twice a day by including them in your morning and afternoon routines.

This way, all your Speedies are completed without extra effort or stress, as you're batching them and keeping your Task Management system uncluttered.

However, if you prefer, add them to your end-of-day routine.

Remember, it's your Task Management system. Tailor it to your needs, build it, and enjoy it!

2.3.2 PROJECT MANAGEMENT

"Nobody is perfect, but a team can be." — Meredith Belbin

At this point, you've done a great job designing and organizing your personal world, being able to perfectly take care of all the information and actions that come your way.

Now, it's the perfect moment to bring the same order and effectiveness to your whole team.

Following the ICOR® Framework's guidance, we've already covered PKM (Personal Knowledge Management) and PPM (Personal Project Management or, if you prefer, Task Management).

Now, we'll conquer BKM (Business Knowledge Management) and BPM (Business Project Management).

In the next chapters, you'll grasp how to communicate effectively, create an expansive productivity system, mitigate disruptions, work asynchronously, and enable your team to focus and deliver outcomes swiftly without undue stress.

Here are some highlights of what's in store:

- Become proficient in planning and attaining goals.
- Dive deep into advanced priority-setting techniques.
- Streamline the process of turning brilliant ideas into tangible results.
- Enhance how your team interacts and communicates.

We'll start with the basic concepts, like defining what we mean by Project Management. Setting clear boundaries is key, so you don't get lost.

Next, we'll introduce you to the Output Elements, the basic

units and building blocks of your Project Management system.

We'll finish our key concepts explanation with PEA (Plan, Execute, Align), our powerful mental model that'll guide your planning and execution process to ensure alignment with your goals.

Once you've got these concepts clear, you'll be ready to dive deep into the workflows you need to put all these concepts into practice.

Firstly, meet The Execution Beast, our crucial mental model in the world of action in the business area, to transition from creating Output Elements to planning and executing them through PEA.

Next, we introduce The Idea Incubator, a transformative mental model that aids in converting any bright spark or idea into powerful actions, leading to remarkable outcomes and tangible results.

Lastly, discover how to design, build and implement an extraordinary and exceptional Communication Management system. A system enveloped in transparency and trust, thriving on asynchronous teamwork, and planted firmly in a core ICOR® concept: the Single Source of Truth.

We're thrilled and can't wait to share with you all this knowledge!

2.3.2.1 CONCEPTS

2.3.2.1.1 THE PUZZLE OF PROJECT MANAGEMENT: PIECE BY PIECE

"We must give a lot of thought to the future because that is where we are going to spend the rest of our lives." — *John Maynard Keynes*

B efore we move on, it's essential to define this seemingly "enigmatic" concept: Project Management.

Have you ever wondered what Project Management really means?

We consider Project Management an art, much like conducting an orchestra.

It's about effectively leading your team, ensuring everything goes smoothly, finishes on time, and that the experience is stress-free for everyone.

When applied correctly, Project Management empowers every team member to contribute productively towards the team's shared goals. But that's not all; it also refines the framework of their interactions, enriching conversations and boosting the overall collaborative vibe.

So, what exactly does Project Management encompass?

Let's break it down:

- It's about plotting and arranging everyone's tasks, like pieces of a complex puzzle, ensuring your projects stay on the right path.
- It involves assigning priorities to tasks, a bit like a strategic game of chess, making sure the critical steps are tackled promptly.
- It's focused on aligning each player's moves with the overall strategy, connecting individual tasks to the team's goals for a harmonious flow.
- It requires the magic of transforming wild, creative ideas into solid, workable steps that everyone on the team can bring to life.

- Above all, it's about strengthening the bonds of communication, establishing effective communication channels between team members for seamless collaboration.

These aspects weave the tapestry of Project Management, a dynamic blend of strategic planning, effective communication, and unified teamwork to turn any goal into an achievable reality.

A Project Management system is basically your toolbox, chosen from a wide array of concepts and workflows to help you manage your team's tasks proficiently. It's about how you put these concepts to work using the software tools you find most helpful.

Think of your Project Management system as the nerve center, steering the course of your team.

It's the go-to platform where everyone stays updated on how things are progressing.

It's the place where tasks are understood, questions are answered, and conversations are sparked, all geared towards propelling your team closer to its goals.

In the next chapters, we'll guide you through setting up your own Project Management system, which touches on all these aspects.

2.3.2.1.2 OUTPUT ELEMENTS UNVEILED: ORGANIZING AND SIMPLIFYING PROJECT MANAGEMENT

"The biggest goal can be achieved if you simply break it down into enough small parts." — Henry Ford

A s we've previously discussed, Project Management revolves around understanding and organizing your team's numerous and often complex tasks.

To simplify this process, we've developed the Output Elements, a set of objects designed to streamline these tasks.

The Output Elements are divided into two main categories:

- Actionable elements.
- Non-actionable elements.

Actionable elements require execution to produce deliverables, while non-actionable elements serve as containers, organizational objects, providing clarity and helping you switch between broad overviews and detailed analyses.

In ICOR®, as you already know, there's only one actionable Output Element: the Task.

A Task is something someone needs to complete.

We've already discussed how you tackle tasks, but it's important enough that we're going to review it once more and focus on the key points you should remember.

A Task can range from a quick 15-minute job to something that takes up to three hours. Tasks under 15 minutes are called Speedies.

Two critical aspects of tasks are:

1. **Planning**. You need to define when the Task will be executed.
2. **Outcome**. You need to identify what the Task will achieve or produce like, for example, a script or report.

We recommend starting each Task name with an action verb like, for example: Create, Design, Write, Call, or Edit. This practice helps in several ways:

- Quickly identifies tasks in your Project Management system.
- Forces you to be specific about the expected outcome.
- Motivates the person responsible to take action on it.

If tasks need to be broken down into smaller steps, you can use subtasks.

In that case, you should name the initial Task to reflect the overall outcome; then use action verbs for the subtasks to maintain and ensure clarity in the Task and subtask structure.

For example, if you start with a Task named "Create monthly sales report" and realize there are many actions involved, you can create a Task named "Monthly sales report" with the following subtasks:

- Export data from the ERP (Enterprise Resource Planning software, a type of software that businesses use to manage day-to-day activities such as accounting).
- Create Excel file.
- Prepare presentation.

As you can see, the initial Task becomes a container, with the real work (the actionable elements) being done in the subtasks.

We also recommend using capital letters to easily identify container tasks. This technique, along with removing the verb, makes identification simple. In this case, the initial "Create monthly sales report" would be converted to "MONTHLY SALES REPORT."

But, you can also use and take advantage of other Output Elements to create containers:

- Goals
- Projects
- Workstreams
- Operations

Understanding Goals in ICOR® means seeing them not just as targets to achieve but also as guiding paths to follow.

This perspective keeps your Project Management system adaptable and flexible, allowing you to embrace new opportunities without losing focus.

Goals offer a stable direction and a clear "path to follow," organizing all tasks to align with the overall direction.

Projects, Workstreams, and Operations help group related tasks and ensure they align with one or more goals:

- **Projects** encapsulate one-time activities with a clear start and end date, leading to a specific outcome. For example, designing a product, which concludes with the final design.
- **Workstreams** consist of ongoing, repetitive tasks executed sequentially. Content creation, like producing YouTube videos, fits here, where each cycle follows the same steps.
- **Operations** cover tasks outside the scope of Projects and Workstreams, such as administrative duties or unique asset creation.

This structured approach creates a three-level hierarchical system:

1. **Level 1**. Goals.
2. **Level 2**. Projects, Workstreams, or Operations.
3. **Level 3**. Tasks.

These three levels let you move up and down easily, offering a bird's eye view from the top and a detailed look at the tiniest details in Level 3 for any action item you need to complete.

2.3.2.1.3 HARNESSING ICOR®'S FLEXIBILITY: THE OUTPUT FORMULA

"It always seems impossible until it's done." — Nelson Mandela

I COR®'s standout feature is its flexibility, allowing you to apply it to any software tool on the market. This adaptability extends to every element of the methodology, including the Output Elements and the Output Formula.

The Output Formula empowers you to create your Output Elements using two main approaches: Bottom-Up and Top-Down.

Let's explore each one in detail.

In the Bottom-Up approach, you start with a clear and specific action, known as a Task.

This approach begins with certainty, knowing exactly what needs to be done. However, tasks can evolve and become more complex over time.

If a Task becomes complicated, you might initially break it down into subtasks, as discussed in the previous chapter.

If the complexity increases further, you create more tasks and group them under higher-level Output Elements, such as Projects, Workstreams, or Operations, depending on the nature of the tasks.

As you progress, things might get even more complicated, and you could start losing perspective. This is when you turn to the highest object in the Output Element's hierarchy: a Goal.

Defining a Goal provides a clear perspective of your ultimate purpose, assembling all underlying Projects, Workstreams, Operations, and their associated tasks.

This process streamlines the Bottom-Up approach within the Output Formula.

But, what if you need to approach things differently?

That's where the Top-Down approach comes in, perfect for when you're starting with a broad, abstract concept.

This uncertainty often leaves you wondering where to start. Begin by setting a clear Goal, something you want to achieve or at least a direction you'd like to head in.

From this broad vision, you identify significant actions required to accomplish this goal.

These big actions help define broader categories of effort, focusing on Projects, Workstreams, or Operations.

By concentrating on these Output Elements, specific and manageable tasks naturally emerge. These tasks are easy to manage and have defined outcomes, making them straightforward and efficient for any team member to execute.

It's important to note that the Top-Down and Bottom-Up approaches aren't limited to navigating from goals to tasks or vice versa. This dynamic approach can also be applied flexibly between tasks and subtasks, adapting to real-time needs and insights.

In summary, ICOR®'s flexibility allows you to effectively manage and execute your projects, whether you start with a specific task or a broad goal. This adaptability ensures that you can tailor the methodology to fit any situation, enhancing productivity and achieving your goals efficiently.

2.3.2.1.4 THE PEA REVOLUTION: TRANSFORMING HOW YOU SET PRIORITIES

If you have more than three priorities, you don't have any." —Jim Collins

We designed and developed PEA to streamline setting priorities in your Project Management system with a radically different approach.

PEA stands for Plan, Execute, Align. It's the mental model we use to handle priorities, moving away from traditional labels like high, medium, or low, and avoiding numbering them as one, two, three, etc.

We found the old-school method confusing and, frankly, ineffective. People often got stuck trying to differentiate a "medium" from a "low" priority task.

This system also implied that only high-priority tasks were important, leaving low and medium-priority tasks overlooked.

That's a risky oversight because often it's the accumulation of these so-called "low-priority" tasks that build the foundation for significant achievements over time in any business and in any busy professional's life.

Getting your priorities straight is really about mastering Time Management. And that's what we'll do.

Essentially, priorities help you determine the "when" of actions.

When you use the high, medium, and low approach, you're really saying and meaning you should focus first on your high-priority tasks, then the medium-priority ones, and finally the low-priority ones.

In the world of Task Management and Project Management, we consider you just need straightforward answers to these three questions:

1. WHEN am I going to do this?
2. WHAT do I do now?
3. Am I doing what I SHOULD be doing?

If you have clear and immediate answers to these, your Task Management and Project Management Systems are running perfectly. You have full control over your action world.

And that's where PEA comes into play:

- **Plan** tackles, "WHEN am I going to do this?"
- **Execute** addresses, "WHAT do I do now?"
- **Align** ensures you're checking, "Am I doing what I SHOULD be doing?"

By recognizing that priorities are really about Time Management, you set the stage for success.

In the coming chapters, we'll dive deeper into this concept, explaining the workflows that help you master your priorities without any second-guessing.

2.3.2.2 WORKFLOWS

"Well begun is half done." — Aristotle

I n this section, we're shifting gears from useful theory (concepts) to practical use (workflows).

We'll take the insights from the concepts we've previously explained and show you how to apply them, breaking down the essential steps to craft your ultimate Project Management System.

We'll start introducing The Execution Beast.

This isn't just a workflow; it's your game plan.

We'll guide you on how to create your Output Elements and, more importantly, how to bring them to life using PEA.

The Execution Beast is your go-to strategy for keeping everything you do tightly aligned with your ultimate goals. It's about mastering the art of planning and taking action in a way that ensures your team's tasks and goals are always in harmony, keeping you and your team on the right track.

Next, we'll dive into The Idea Incubator.

Ideas are easy to come by, but executing them is a whole different game.

The Idea Incubator mental model is your tool for capturing those ideas, evaluating their worth with your team, and integrating the valuable ones into The Execution Beast. This way, no golden opportunity slips away, and you systematically assess the feasibility of each new spark.

We'll wrap up this section by explaining how to build a perfect Team Communication Management system.

Imagine your team in perfect sync, with information flowing

seamlessly and minimal distractions. That's what a solid Team Communication Management system offers.

We'll also help you establish a Business Knowledge Management (BKM) system, anchored on our core principle Single Source of Truth.

It's about building a hub where every piece of information, every action item, and all communication lives and can be retrieved without hassle.

By integrating these three components, you're not just managing projects; you're leading a dynamic, high-performance Project Management system, perfectly integrated with your productivity system end to end.

Your team won't just be working; they'll be synergizing, hitting peak performance levels, and achieving goals without burnout.

Let's dive in and transform your Project Management into a powerhouse system!

2.3.2.2.1 UNLOCKING YOUR POTENTIAL: MEET THE EXECUTION BEAST

"Action is the foundational key to all success." — Pablo Picasso

A s you already know, ICOR® breaks down productivity into two different worlds: Information and Action.

Now, we're at that crucial point where everything we've been working on comes together seamlessly, like pieces of a puzzle fitting perfectly into place.

Remember when we discussed the PKM system and The Capturing Beast?

This mental model helps you capture essential information using the "Current Projects - Key Elements - Topics" approach.

Capturing information is just the beginning; the first step in running your productivity system.

ICOR® has been deeply thought and designed to guide you through building a complete productivity system end to end. This means capturing and processing information isn't enough. You need to transform that information into actions that move you closer to your goals.

That's why we created another mental model called The Execution Beast.

The Execution Beast addresses a problem that has challenged businesses throughout history: connecting strategy with its implementation.

The Execution Beast is where Project Management and Task Management merge into one cohesive system; the perfect Output system, where everything fits together and runs like a well-oiled machine.

Here's where you'll see how every individual's daily work contributes to the team's main goals and the business as a whole, creating a powerful alignment between Goals and daily tasks.

The Execution Beast simplifies this alignment with two straightforward steps:

1. Creating the initial Output Elements.
2. Using PEA (Plan, Execute, Align) to make sure every task you tackle moves you closer to your Goals.

Let's dive in and start with a bold statement: Forget annual planning. It's outdated.

The world has changed drastically, and so has how we should approach productivity. That's what ICOR® does.

Opportunities arise constantly, so we need a productivity system that allows us to plan and execute quickly.

Instead of annual planning, we focus on quarterly planning to develop the initial Output Elements.

If your company still uses annual planning, don't worry. You can align your quarterly goals with the yearly ones, showing that you're consistently working toward them and perfectly justifying your approach.

So, each quarter, set clear and specific Goals to ensure the business outcomes are well-defined.

From these Goals, outline Projects, Workstreams, or Operations that drive the business forward.

Set start and end dates, and if possible, identify specific tasks for those Projects, Workstreams, or Operations.

Each week, plan and execute these tasks using the PEA mental model.

You can also create additional Output Elements during your Weekly or Daily planning as needed.

With your Output Elements set, it's time to engage the second stage of The Execution Beast: PEA.

This mental model answers three crucial questions that any productivity system should always be able to answer for the team and each member:

- When am I going to do this? (Plan)
- What do I do now? (Execute)
- Am I doing what I should be doing? (Align)

When every team member can quickly answer these questions, you can trust that the team will complete all the tasks needed to reach the Goals.

Weekly Planning is essential for keeping the team's efforts streamlined and on track. It involves:

- Setting clear Weekly Goals and tasks that the team commits to completing. These aren't just to-do items: they're commitments!
- Assigning specific days for each task to ensure the plan is realistic, aiming for one Weekly Goal per day (the Highlight of the Day) per team member.
- If there's an overload, the team should decide which tasks can be moved to the next week.

The Weekly Planning should be discussed during The Agenda Meeting.

We strongly recommend scheduling this meeting on the same day and time every week to build a consistent habit; after all, habits are the foundation of any successful system.

Weekly Planning answers our first question: "When am I going to do this?"

But, it's also the crucial link between the business's strategic Goals and each team member's daily tasks.

From Weekly Planning, we move smoothly into Daily Execution, transitioning from Project Management to Task Management without friction.

This natural flow ensures everyone understands why they are doing what they are doing, which is key to maintaining a motivated and engaged team.

So, how should each team member execute that perfectly drawn plan?

For effective Daily Execution, each team member needs to pay attention simultaneously to four key variables before tackling any task: Energy Level, Urgency, Speedies, and Unexpected Events.

Though it may seem complex at first, practicing this daily will make it second nature because it's rooted in common sense.

Let's break them down.

First, **Energy Level**.

Each team member should schedule their Deep Work tasks when they're at peak performance, usually in the morning when energy is highest.

This task should be the Highlight of the Day, one of the Weekly Goals planned in the Agenda Meeting.

Doing it first thing ensures it gets done, which not only moves the team closer to their Goals but also boosts motivation for the rest of the day.

Positioning this task at the top of the planner answers the question, "What do I do now?"

Next, let's talk about **Urgency**.

Not everything is "urgent."

Urgent tasks are those that have a significant impact on the business. If it's not done immediately, it will cause major problems.

If a task doesn't meet these criteria, it's not urgent, so the person should stick to the priorities set during the Agenda Meeting, guided by the Weekly Goals.

Understanding and internalizing what "urgent" really means helps avoid unnecessary interruptions, allowing the team to work asynchronously and perform at peak levels.

Now, onto **Speedies**.

These are under-15-minute tasks that pop up frequently.

While it's tempting to tackle them immediately, it's better to capture them and address them during scheduled times. Batching these tasks ensures high performance and helps manage small chunks of time effectively.

For example, if any team member has a 30-minute slot that doesn't fit any planned tasks, he should use it to knock out a few Speedies. This smart use of time helps reduce the load during regular daily routines.

Finally, we come to **Unexpected Events**.

When an Unexpected Event arises, the team member should decide between his current task and this new "unexpected guest."

The key is to choose the task that is more important for the Goals and today's plan. This decision-making process simplifies work life by making it easier to prioritize.

In PEA, planning and executing are sequential processes, but alignment happens naturally.

When the team clearly sets up Output Elements and plans one

Weekly Goal (The Highlight of the Day) each day for each team member, everyone is always moving towards the business Goals, driven by a clear sense of purpose, and that makes all the difference!

This approach removes the pressure, allowing team members to focus solely on executing, knowing they're doing what they should be doing at any moment, no matter the circumstances.

We strongly recommend revisiting alignment during each Agenda Meeting to ensure tasks and Goals are always aligned, making any necessary adjustments to stay on track.

2.3.2.2.2 TURNING FLEETING THOUGHTS INTO TANGIBLE RESULTS: THE IDEA INCUBATOR

"There's no shortage of remarkable ideas; what's missing is the will to execute them." — *Seth Godin*

A successful Project Management system must never overlook a crucial aspect: no idea, no matter how small, should ever be ignored.

Ideas are the powerhouse of a team's progress, and neglecting them is a luxury no business or busy professional can afford.

However, transitioning from the abstract (an idea) to the concrete (action and implementation) isn't always straightforward.

This challenge inspired us to design and develop The Idea Incubator, a mental model within our Project Management system that streamlines the journey from fleeting thoughts to tangible results in just four clear steps: Capture, Evaluate, Plan, and Execute.

The Idea Incubator is also a perfect opportunity to explore the concept of Single Source of Truth (SSOT) more deeply.

We strongly recommend reading this chapter carefully, as it will give you a clearer understanding of just how powerful this concept can be.

SSOT is a nuanced concept, and it's easy to miss its full potential if you don't pay close attention to the details. Many busy professionals might overlook these finer points, missing out on all the features and benefits it offers. By diving into real-world examples in this chapter, you'll gain a much better grasp of the entire concept.

Let's dive in!

Ideas can strike at any moment, so it's crucial to have a dedicated space where you can easily capture and retrieve them. This space becomes your SSOT for all ideas in your Project Management system, playing a key role in The Idea Incubator.

You'll soon see that the SSOT isn't just a place to store ideas; it's a flexible and dynamic concept that can elevate your Project Management system to new heights.

When someone adds a new idea to the SSOT, that idea itself becomes the SSOT for others to build on.

This is so because it ensures that all team members know where to add their thoughts and feedback, allowing the idea to grow, evolve, and improve.

This is how the Capture step turns the SSOT into a hub for innovation, unlocking the full potential of ideas by keeping them well-defined, clearly identified and richly contextualized.

After capturing the idea, it's time to move to the next step: Evaluate.

Not all ideas will fit your immediate goals, which is why evaluation is key. Integrating regular review routines helps your system run efficiently, almost on autopilot, saving you from manual hassle.

We highly recommend, at least, a quarterly review where every idea is considered and classified as either To be planned, Someday, or Rejected.

To be planned ideas need immediate attention and should be swiftly transitioned to The Execution Beast, creating the necessary Output Elements you may consider.

Someday ideas aren't a priority but hold potential and require periodic re-evaluation, which we suggest doing quarterly too.

Finally, Rejected ideas are those that, upon assessment, do not serve the team's goals or the business strategy.

After evaluating your ideas, it's time to move to the third and fourth steps: Plan and Execute.

You need to move those To be planned ideas to The Execution Beast, following the same steps as any other action.

Pay attention to the idea's business impact and implementation timeline, as ideas can be great opportunities but also risky elements in your planning and goals.

If an idea promises significant impact and demands a short execution time, it should be fast-tracked into your Weekly Goals. This flexibility ensures that valuable ideas are quickly executed and completed.

For ideas that require a longer execution time, follow the same steps outlined in The Execution Beast.

That's the result of a well-polished productivity system. You're always using the same workflows you've already thought out, designed, and implemented.

In conclusion, the beauty of a robust productivity system lies in its simplicity and ease of use. If your productivity system is based on workflows like those in The Idea Incubator, it becomes a system you run on autopilot, guiding your team and you toward swift goal achievement.

We encourage you to observe, internalize, and incorporate these strategies and workflows into your professional life. It's not just about getting things done; it's about achieving more with less effort, stress, and time.

That's the power of a productivity system that genuinely works for you.

2.3.2.2.3 MAXIMIZING ASYNCHRONOUS PROJECT MANAGEMENT: THE TEAM COMMUNICATION SYSTEM

"Talent wins games, but teamwork and intelligence win championships." — Michael Jordan

The Team Communication system is designed to make communication between team members as smooth as possible.

Its main goal is to continuously optimize, improve, promote, and encourage efficiency, driving the team to achieve peak performance and reach its highest level of productivity.

To get the most out of the Team Communication system and achieve this efficiency, it's essential to let team members work asynchronously. This allows them to focus on their tasks without interruptions, maximizing their time and quickly accessing any information or action they need at any moment.

To guide you in designing and building an effective Team Communication system, we'll focus on two key approaches:

1. Avoid interruptions.
2. Adopt, internalize, and use the concept of Single Source of Truth (SSOT).

Let's explore these approaches in detail.

Approach 1: Avoiding interruptions.

The key to avoiding interruptions is to create and implement communication protocols that every team member not only understands but uses daily.

These protocols guide behavior and help avoid the instinct to interrupt, which often feels like the quickest way to solve a problem but can actually hinder productivity.

We'll introduce two simple protocols that can instantly transform your team's behavior, making interruptions disappear right away:

1. Communication channels.
2. Agenda Meeting.

Let's analyze each of them.

Before reaching out to a colleague, each team member should follow a specific sequence of communication channels:

1. Email or Project Management comments.
2. Messaging.
3. Phone calls.
4. In-Person interactions.

Let's see them one by one.

Email or Project Management comments should be the first option, allowing team members to add context to their requests without causing immediate disruption.

At the Paperless Movement®, we prefer comments in our Project Management system over email, as they keep all relevant information in one place and reduce unnecessary email clutter.

It's essential that the team agrees on a specific timeframe for responding to these comments, such as, for example, within

12 to 24 hours.

This commitment ensures that every request will be addressed within a predictable period, giving team members peace of mind knowing their needs will be met without the need for immediate interruption.

If the situation requires a faster response than this timeframe allows, that's when we move to the next communication channel: messaging.

Without clear guidelines for messaging, interruptions become inevitable, leading to cluttered messaging systems, distractions, inefficiency, and reduced productivity.

The messaging system should be used when a team member needs a response faster than what's expected via email or comments in the Project Management system.

It's also important to include context in every message to avoid confusion, especially when someone revisits the conversation months later.

You can easily provide context by linking related items from your Project Management system and always keeping discussions within their threads.

Threads are crucial for keeping conversations clear and on track, no matter when someone joins in. They help ensure that everyone is on the same page, making them a reliable go-to resource, as we'll explore later.

Teams should also agree on a maximum response time for messages in this system, ideally shorter than what's expected for emails or comments; for instance, within six hours.

To make the messaging system more effective, you can add some simple cues. At the Paperless Movement®, for example:

- We've established a protocol where all messages

generally require a response within six hours.

- An orange dot at the beginning of a message signals that the recipient should reply as soon as they finish their current task or meeting.
- A red dot indicates urgency, meaning the recipient should interrupt their work to respond immediately. These urgent messages perfectly align with The Execution Beast.

This protocol based on emails, comments, and messages allows the team to work asynchronously, maintaining focus on tasks unless something truly urgent arises.

While we prefer asynchronous communication, we understand that busy professionals have packed schedules, so traditional channels like phone calls and in-person interactions are still valuable. However, we approach these channels differently, always betting on working asynchronously.

We only make phone calls when it's truly necessary: when a quick conversation is more effective than writing. Sometimes, a quick conversation can be more efficient than a long string of messages, which can end up wasting time and energy.

However, there's a downside to relying too much on calls: if you don't document the information discussed, your system may become outdated. This, in turn, could push your team back toward the very thing we're trying to avoid: more calls or meetings to catch up on what was missed.

We also believe in the importance of physical interaction when a phone conversation just isn't enough.

Sometimes, face-to-face communication is essential because we're human, and it adds depth to our conversations. However, we approach this differently too.

When someone visits a colleague's desk, it's because it's

absolutely necessary; something urgent that can't wait and requires in-person discussion. With the new protocol we're introducing, these situations will become rare, and unexpected "desk drop-ins" will be a thing of the past.

Instead, we prioritize meetings, but we handle them in a new way.

When a team member feels something needs to be discussed in person, they add it to the Agenda Meeting item in our Project Management system. This allows us to gather all topics in one weekly meeting rather than scattering multiple meetings throughout the week.

So, rather than interrupting a colleague with every new thought, each team member takes a moment to assess its importance. If it's still relevant, it gets added to the Agenda Meeting for discussion during our Weekly Planning.

By just adopting these two protocols (communication channels and Agenda Meeting), your team can minimize disruptions, consolidate discussions and decisions, and ensure everyone is on the same page when they need the team's input.

Approach 2: Having a SSOT.

At the start of this book, we introduced the SSOT as a key concept. Now, we'll show you how powerful and transformative this idea can be for your team.

When every team member fully grasps the concept of SSOT, it greatly enhances asynchronous work for two main reasons:

1. **It minimizes interruptions** because everyone knows exactly where to create and store any information or action within the Project Management system.
2. **It drastically cuts down the time spent searching for and retrieving information or actions**. Consider this: Imagine how much time you could save by having

everything organized and easily accessible.

With a well-defined SSOT, everything is exactly where it should be, so team members don't need to interrupt each other to find what they need.

By exploring several best practices, you'll not only solidify your understanding of SSOT but also learn how to implement it effectively within your team.

Here are the ones we strongly recommend you start using today to take your team's performance, literally, to the next level:

- **Include a "To Review" stage or status in your tasks**. When a task reaches this point, it signals that it's ready for feedback. A designated reviewer can then provide input, making this task the go-to place for all related discussions. This way, any team member can find the context they need without having to ask others, centralizing feedback and discussions asynchronously. It also allows task owners and assignees to focus on other tasks until feedback is needed or provided.
- **Centralize Output Elements**. Every Output Element the team creates in the Project Management system should become a SSOT. This ensures that all relevant information is centralized, allowing everyone to contribute confidently, knowing that they are all on the same page.
- **Respect conversation threads**. Maintaining structured discussion threads in your Project Management system ensures that conversations are organized and easy to follow. Each thread becomes the SSOT for that topic, allowing anyone to quickly catch up on the discussion without missing important details.

- **Use custom views**. Finally, custom views in your Project Management system can be incredibly valuable. For example, a view that displays Weekly Goals helps keep everyone aligned and focused on the priorities for that week. This view acts as the SSOT for the team's focus, making sure everyone knows the progress and goals for the week.

When these protocols and best practices are integrated effectively, they streamline an asynchronous Project Management system, boosting individual and collective productivity.

A strong Project Management system, combined with these practices, empowers teams to reach their full potential, even in the face of challenges.

This infrastructure fosters trust and focus, enabling team members to concentrate on what truly matters: execution.

2. 4 STAGE 4: REFINE

"I'm a slow walker, but I never walk back." — Abraham Lincoln

H ere, we enter your gateway to the final stage of ICOR®: Refine.

It's easy to overlook refining your productivity system after setting it up, but it's a crucial step to truly elevate your productivity, as you will soon discover.

Remember these two important points:

- Real transformation happens in this stage.
- Always keep in mind that refining your productivity system is an ongoing process. It's something you should continuously do to consistently improve your work and perform at your best without burning out.

In this section of the book, you'll learn the essence of Refine, its key concepts, and essential workflows, helping you achieve a productivity system that's not only efficient but also operating at its peak.

But, before we dive in, let's break down Refine's two main steps: Optimize and Automate.

Optimize is about enhancing functionality and simplifying processes, while Automate focuses on seamless execution, putting your productivity system on autopilot.

When optimizing, your goals are threefold:

1. Eliminate redundancies.
2. Streamline processes.
3. Enhance efficiency.

Once optimization is in place, you can then focus on automation.

Often misunderstood as solely software-driven, automation extends far beyond that "simple" approach, as you will see in the upcoming chapters. It involves two crucial concepts:

1. **Sequentiality**. Aligning processes to be executed one after another, avoiding multitasking.
2. **Repetition**. Implementing repetitive workflows for a more automated system.

Most people think their productivity system is complete and finished once they've mastered information and action.

But, it's this stage, Refine, that truly distinguishes a "pro" productivity system, as it merges the best of information and action, ICOR®'s two main worlds, and elevates them even further.

As you know, a productivity system isn't just about the tools you use. It's mainly about concepts and workflows. Once these are in place, refining them is not just beneficial: it becomes essential!

So, let's make this happen! Let's refine your productivity system to its utmost potential!

2.4.1 CONCEPTS

2.4.1.1 WHAT OPTIMIZATION REALLY MEANS: THE SECRETS OF BATCHING, MOMENTUM, AND FOCUS

"Perfection is not attainable, but if we chase perfection we can catch excellence." — Vince Lombardi

O ptimization and simplification are often mistaken for one another, but they are distinct concepts.

Simplification aims to make things easier, while Optimization focuses on enhancing efficiency.

To enhance your workflows and boost efficiency, let's explore three effective strategies.

First up is Batching.

This means grouping similar tasks and completing them together. Think of activities like emails, administrative tasks, or meetings.

By scheduling these tasks for specific times, you can develop daily Routines that handle them all at once, streamlining your processes and effectively putting them on autopilot.

This way, your productivity system guides you on when to tackle these batched tasks without even thinking, rather than the tasks dictating your schedule.

Next is Momentum.

This involves seizing the moment and adapting plans to current situations for better and faster results.

Embracing Momentum can significantly boost productivity, which is why we've dedicated an entire chapter to it.

Lastly, Focus is crucial for Optimization. Fully concentrating on a task can dramatically improve performance, allowing you to achieve peak levels effortlessly.

While there are many ways to boost Optimization, concentrating on these three strategies (Batching, Momentum, and Focus) will significantly enhance your productivity system and overall performance.

Remember, in productivity and in life, less is often more.

2.4.1.2 BEYOND SOFTWARE: RUNNING ON AUTOPILOT WITH AUTOMATION

"The more we value things outside our control, the less control we have." — Marcus Aurelius

A s we've previously mentioned, most people think Automation is just about software doing tasks on its own. But Automation is much more than that: It's about streamlining tasks in all areas of our lives.

To help you better understand how to approach Automation, we'll outline three key strategies.

First, there's the concept of "running things on autopilot."

This means treating yourself like a system, shaped by habits and daily Routines that run smoothly and intuitively. When you respond instinctively to familiar situations, you use your intuition to make your work easier and more efficient.

The second approach is the more traditional one: using software to handle background processes.

Today, almost all software includes some form of automation. For example, software tools like Zapier are designed specifically for this purpose.

Finally, the third approach is Artificial Intelligence (AI).

AI is transforming how we interact with information and take action. This cutting-edge technology manages complex tasks, giving you more time and energy to focus on what you do best: thinking.

It's important to keep refining your productivity system by building workflows that are logical and intuitive; the ones that make sense to you.

Your productivity system should always reflect how your brain works, ensuring it's sustainable and effective over time.

Aim to create a productivity system that runs on autopilot, so you can reclaim your most valuable asset: your time.

2.4.1.3 RIDE THE WAVE: HOW MOMENTUM TRANSFORMS YOUR WORKDAY

"Momentum solves 80% of your problems." — John C. Maxwell

I n this chapter, we'll explore a transformative concept in planning and productivity: Momentum.

At the Paperless Movement®, we define productivity or being productive as "performing at your best without burning out."

It's not just about outcomes or deliverables; it's about maximizing your time efficiently.

When you consistently perform at your best, results naturally follow. These results reflect how well you execute tasks.

A solid productivity system is invaluable. Once established, it operates smoothly on its own, ensuring you achieve your goals through efficient task completion.

But what exactly is Momentum?

Momentum means motion, action, getting things done, and entering the famous "flow state."

In this state, you experience five key elements:

1. Complete focus on the task.
2. Mental clarity.
3. A serene mindset free from external worries.
4. Timelessness that immerses you in the present.
5. Heightened motivation and energized productivity.

So, how does Momentum manifest?

It's not something you actively seek; it emerges spontaneously. When it does, it prompts you to set aside your plans and follow its lead.

The result is often completing more work of higher quality in less time than you anticipated.

This efficiency is due to Momentum's inherent features: increased speed and improved outcomes, enabling faster task completion in a state of flow and yielding superior results due to intense focus and concentration.

However, Momentum cannot be scheduled. So, how should you handle it?

There are two rules to remember:

1. When you feel compelled to do something, go for it, letting Momentum guide you. But be cautious, as Momentum has its downsides the moment you take it to extremes. For example, it can lead to procrastination.
2. Apply Momentum only to critical tasks aligned with your major goals.

One final conclusion: While it's essential to plan and stay organized, be ready to re-plan around Momentum to fully leverage its benefits.

2.4.1.4 THE ESSENCE OF ICOR®: FINDING JOY AND PURPOSE IN PRODUCTIVITY

"You've already achieved goals you said would make you happy." — Alex Hormozi

I n this chapter, we're taking a slight detour from our usual topics on information and action, diving into the more philosophical and existential, but necessary, aspects of productivity.

This shift is crucial in the Refine stage of ICOR®.

Have you ever wondered why you do the things you do?

For us, the answer is simple: it brings us joy.

It's important to not only love what you do but also find meaning in it; a sense of purpose.

That's why we say ICOR® is more than just a methodology. It gives meaning and justifies why you should design and build a productivity system end to end.

In our fast-paced world, we often overlook these essential questions, getting swept up in the current of life where productivity can be quick but chaotic.

When you find yourself in this whirlwind, try reframing your perspective: If you're only doing important things, shouldn't every day feel great?

This is the essence of ICOR®: making sense of it all by focusing on what truly matters and finding satisfaction in that success.

ICOR® is a set of concepts and workflows designed to manage information and action, ensuring you spend your time on what's most important to YOU.

It's about moving YOU from goals to achievements, leading YOU to a work and life of fulfillment, joy, and happiness, as you will always be acting on YOUR own criteria and YOUR common sense.

ICOR® also helps in controlling emotions and handling sensations.

In today's high-pressure work environment, it's easy to end up with anxiety, stress, or even depression. By mastering ICOR®, you can navigate and even eliminate these negative emotions, as ICOR® gives you control over your work, leading to relaxation, calm, and peace of mind.

This positive feedback loop enhances your performance, leading to better outcomes and closer alignment with your goals.

Contrary to the belief held by some, especially in the corporate world, that immense pressure is needed for peak performance, we believe that our best state to perform at a peak level is one of relaxation, calmness, and focus.

It's in this state of mind that we find clarity, bringing out our best.

2.4.1.5 ELEVATE YOUR BUSINESS BEYOND BASICS: PROCESSES, WORKFLOWS, WORKSTREAMS, PROCEDURES, AND SOPS

"The secret of success is to do the common things uncommonly well." — John D. Rockefeller

When we discussed Project Management, we introduced you to the Output Elements, objects designed to streamline your tasks for better planning and execution.

Now, we'll take this concept a step further by exploring additional essential elements that will help you understand, organize, and refine your business processes.

These elements will further illuminate the two core worlds in ICOR®: Information and Action.

You'll see that ICOR® isn't just for you or your team: it can be applied across the whole company or business!

But first, you need to understand what a business process is.

Simply put, a business process, which we'll refer to as Process, is an organized task performed by people or machines to achieve a specific business goal. These processes can range from simple to complex tasks.

As processes become more complex, we introduce another element: a Workflow.

A Workflow is a collection of processes that provides a broader perspective, helping you understand the inputs and outputs of complex tasks.

However, businesses are rarely simple.

When workflows become complex, we introduce another element, a Workstream, which acts as a container for these workflows.

But, as you know, ICOR® also covers the world of Information, and business processes are no exception.

ICOR® tackles the information aspect of business processes with two key elements: Procedures and SOPs.

A Procedure is a set of specific instructions for executing a Process, Workflow, or Workstream.

It ensures that anyone can perform these tasks consistently and efficiently, adhering to expected standards.

As with action elements, procedures can become complex. This is where Standard Operating Procedures (SOPs) come in.

SOPs group related procedures, providing comprehensive guidelines for complex tasks.

To make these concepts more relatable and engaging, let's consider a real-world example that's both relevant and common in the business world: corporate travel management.

At the most basic level, a Process involves an employee booking a business trip, following these steps:

1. The employee selects travel dates.
2. He chooses a flight and hotel.
3. He submits the booking request for approval.
4. Once approved, the travel arrangements are finalized.

This simple Process is straightforward and repetitive, suitable for handling individual travel requests.

As the company grows, managing individual travel bookings separately becomes cumbersome, especially when multiple employees are traveling to the same event or location.

A Workflow is introduced to organize these processes into a structured sequence:

1. All travel requests are submitted by employees.
2. The travel coordinator reviews all requests.

3. The coordinator groups requests by destination or event.
4. The coordinator arranges group bookings to optimize cost and logistics.

As you can see, this Workflow connects several processes (booking, approval, coordination) into a cohesive system, making the travel management more efficient.

As the organization expands further, corporate travel becomes more complex, involving international trips, multiple departments, and various types of travel (e.g., sales meetings, conferences, training).

A Workstream is introduced to manage these multiple workflows:

1. Workflow for domestic travel. Handles processes specific to national trips.
2. Workflow for international travel. Manages the added complexities of international bookings, such as visas and currency exchanges.
3. Workflow for event travel. Coordinates large groups attending the same conference or event.

This Workstream allows the company to manage the diverse and growing travel needs efficiently by categorizing different workflows under one umbrella.

Once the world of Action is solved, let's focus on the world of Information.

To ensure consistency, a simple Procedure is developed to guide employees through the steps of submitting a travel request:

1. Access the travel management portal.
2. Fill out the travel request form with required details (dates, destination, purpose).

3. Attach any necessary documents (invitation letters, approvals).
4. Submit the form for approval.

This Procedure ensures that every employee follows the same steps, reducing errors and streamlining the travel booking Process.

Finally, as the travel needs become even more intricate, an SOP is created to provide a comprehensive set of guidelines covering all aspects of corporate travel.

The SOP has these components:

1. **Procedure for booking flights and hotels**. Details the steps to book and get approvals.
2. **Procedure for expense reporting**. Outlines how to report travel expenses and seek reimbursement.
3. **Procedure for handling emergencies abroad**. Provides steps to follow in case of travel-related emergencies.

The SOP combines all relevant procedures into a single document, offering employees and travel coordinators a reference for handling even the most complex travel scenarios efficiently and consistently.

Starting from a simple Process of booking a trip, this example escalates in complexity, justifying the need for workflows to manage related tasks, workstreams to oversee broader categories of travel, procedures to standardize individual tasks, and finally, SOPs to ensure comprehensive and consistent management of the entire travel program.

This structured approach ensures that as the business scales, its travel management remains organized, efficient, and adaptable.

This five-element structure (Process, Workflow, Workstream, Procedure, and SOP) helps efficiently organize any business processes.

It allows for both top-down and bottom-up approaches.

We recommend starting with processes (bottom-up) since it's easier to identify the necessary steps. As complexity grows, group them into workflows and workstreams, as we showed in the previous example.

This approach applies to information elements as well, starting with procedures and building up to SOPs as needed.

Now, equipped with this clear structure of concepts, you're ready to better understand how to make them work.

2.4.2 WORKFLOWS

"Champions keep playing until they get it right." — Billie Jean King

A s you know, the final stage of ICOR®, Refine, involves two pivotal steps: Optimize and Automate.

To optimize and automate effectively, you must first gain a thorough understanding of your business processes, analyzing them as deeply as possible to enhance efficiency.

We believe in simplicity as the foundation. Therefore, we'll focus on just two key approaches to guide you in optimizing and automating your business processes.

Be sure these approaches will literally move your processes to the next level.

The first approach is to identify repetitive processes.

The second one involves examining projects you're currently working on or have recently completed.

Let's explore each of them in detail.

2.4.2.1 AUTOMATE TO INNOVATE: IDENTIFYING AND STREAMLINING REPETITIVE PROCESSES

*"Follow effective action with quiet reflection. From the quiet reflection will come even more effective action." —
Peter Drucker*

One key strategy for boosting productivity is to identify repetitive processes in your business.

When you notice a Process that's done frequently, it presents a golden opportunity for closer examination, optimization, and possibly even automation.

Take a look at the Paperless Movement®, for example.

We have ongoing workstreams dedicated to content creation, such as producing YouTube videos and writing articles. These tasks are done regularly and require a lot of effort to ensure they meet our quality standards.

To maximize efficiency, we've devoted significant time and resources to thoroughly analyzing these processes.

By doing so, we've been able to pinpoint areas where we can streamline operations. This involves breaking down each step of the Process, identifying bottlenecks, and finding ways to simplify, automate, or even outsource those steps.

For instance, in our video production Process, we might look at everything from pre-production planning and scripting to recording and editing.

By evaluating each stage, we can find ways to use technology and tools to speed up these tasks without compromising on quality. This could involve using automation software to handle repetitive editing tasks, outsourcing to specialized companies, or creating templates for common video types.

The benefits of this approach are substantial.

By optimizing and automating repetitive tasks, we've managed to significantly speed up our content generation Process. This not only allows us to produce more content in less time but also frees up our team to focus on more creative and strategic work, ensuring that we maintain our high-quality standards.

The key takeaway here is that by identifying and refining repetitive processes, you can enhance your productivity. It allows you to work smarter, not harder, ultimately leading to better outcomes and a more efficient business.

So, take a closer look at your daily tasks and ask yourself: What repetitive processes can I analyze, optimize, and automate to boost my productivity and improve my business as well?

2.4.2.2 BEYOND THE GRIND: CREATING SELF-RUNNING PROJECTS THROUGH ANALYSIS

"Quality means doing it right when no one is looking." — *Henry Ford*

Imagine a world where your projects practically run themselves, inefficiencies are ironed out, everyone knows exactly what they need to do, and everything runs like a well-oiled machine.

Sounds like a dream, right?

Well, we can assure you that this can become your reality with a strategic approach to project analysis, as we've done it countless times in our own business and with our clients.

One highly effective method involves taking a deep dive into the projects you're currently working on or have recently completed.

Let's break down how this works with an example from our own experience.

When we developed our courses for the ICOR® Journey in our Membership, we didn't just focus on creating high-quality content. We also invested significant time in meticulously analyzing every Process involved during and after the course development.

We scrutinized each step, from initial planning to final delivery.

This thorough analysis was eye-opening. It allowed us to identify inefficiencies, spot unnecessary repetition, and highlight areas where effort was being wasted.

For instance, we found that certain tasks were being repeated across different stages, adding no value but consuming valuable time.

We also discovered that some processes could be automated,

freeing up our team to focus on more critical aspects of course creation.

These insights were invaluable. They shaped how we approached future projects, enabling us to streamline our workflows.

By addressing these inefficiencies and implementing automation where possible, we significantly sped up our course design and delivery Process. Our execution became faster and more precise, enhancing the overall quality of our courses.

The main point here is the importance of spending time to map out your business processes. That's why we provide templates in our Membership, making the most of visual tools like Miro, for example.

This isn't just about identifying what's going wrong. It's about understanding every element of your Workflow. When you know how each part fits together, you can begin to see where improvements can be made.

Optimizing and automating these processes is crucial. It not only saves time and resources but also enhances your productivity system.

Imagine a system that operates almost on autopilot, allowing you to focus on innovation and growth rather than getting bogged down by repetitive tasks.

In conclusion, taking the time to thoroughly analyze your projects can transform your productivity.

By identifying inefficiencies and opportunities for automation, you can streamline your workflows, making your projects more efficient and effective. This approach doesn't just apply to course development; it's a universal strategy that can benefit any business or personal project.

So, start today. Look at your current projects with a critical eye. Analyze each step, identify areas for improvement, and implement changes.

You'll be amazed at how much more productive you can become, achieving better results with less effort.

This is the power of project analysis; a game-changer in your journey to peak productivity.

SECTION 3 - AND NOW, WHAT? REFLECTIONS ON YOUR ICOR® JOURNEY

"Great things never came from comfort zones." — Neil Strauss

C ongratulations on completing your ICOR® Journey!
You've just achieved something remarkable.

Remember when we first introduced the ICOR® Framework at the start of this book?

We encouraged you to map your current tools within it.

Now, having completed your ICOR® Journey, it's the perfect moment to revisit it with fresh insights.

Pause for a moment and appreciate the clarity you now have in navigating the different areas of the ICOR® Framework. You've reached a pivotal point where everything connects.

Go back to your initial setup and review how you placed your tools when you first explored this life-changing framework.

Does everything align as it should?

Are the tools in their rightful places?

Identify any redundancies or gaps, and make the necessary adjustments until your productivity system feels seamless.

Thanks to your ICOR® Journey, you've naturally achieved what we call "intuitive productivity": running workflows effortlessly, guided by your intuition.

But remember, as we mentioned at the beginning, a book alone can't guarantee peak productivity. It's the actions you take, the application of concepts and workflows, that truly matter.

Productivity is a continuous and endless journey. Even we, at the Paperless Movement®, are constantly refining our productivity system, embracing new tools and workflows through ongoing interaction and iteration.

This book serves as your foundation, a static reference point to revisit whenever you need a refresh. But it's just the beginning.

True productivity is dynamic, requiring continuous engagement, collaboration, and adaptation in a rapidly changing world.

That's why we created the Paperless Movement® Membership.

The ICOR® Journey, as part of our Paperless Movement® Membership, offers an immersive experience enriched with exclusive content, including in-depth explanatory videos, over 50 Magic Slides for visual representation of each ICOR® concept and workflow, and invaluable exchanges of ICOR® Frameworks among our engaged community members.

As a member, you'll find practical, time-saving solutions, engage in interactive sessions, and stay up-to-date with the latest software tools, discounts, and news, all crafted to help you excel in a fast-paced, ever-evolving corporate world.

And, for those ready to accelerate even more their progress, we offer our premier product and service: The INNER CIRCLE Program.

The INNER CIRCLE Program is the heart of the Paperless Movement®, where you'll receive live, personalized coaching directly from the authors, Tom Solid and Paco Cantero.

In just one month, you'll fast-track your ICOR® Journey with tailored guidance, in-depth workflow analysis, and real solutions to the work challenges you face every day.

In essence, your journey with ICOR® begins with this book, but we've designed a pathway for you to embrace continuous growth, guiding you toward achieving your highest potential both professionally and personally.

And... thank you. You've given us something far more precious than the cost of this book; you've given us your time. We truly hope the time you've spent reading it brings lasting value for years ahead.

Wishing you all the best!

LET'S ICOR®!

APPENDIX: GLOSSARY OF ICOR® METHODOLOGY TERMS

"Out of intense complexities, intense simplicities emerge." — Winston Churchill

W elcome to the Appendix of our book, where you'll find a comprehensive glossary of terms essential to the ICOR® methodology.

This section is designed to provide you with short, to-the-point, and specific definitions, allowing you to quickly recall what each term means within the context of ICOR® without having to navigate through the entire book.

In this glossary, you'll encounter a variety of terms, including:

- **Pure ICOR® terms**. These are unique to our methodology, such as the names of our multiple mental models.
- **General public terms**. Common terms like "Project" or "Task" that you may have encountered before in your life. These are included to clarify their specific meaning within the ICOR® methodology, helping you to reframe your understanding based on our approach.

Our aim is to ensure that you have a clear and precise understanding of each term as it applies to the ICOR® methodology. Should you wish to explore any term in greater depth, you are encouraged to refer to the relevant chapters within this book.

The ultimate goal of this Appendix is to aid in quick recall and save you time.

As you already know, we want you to have the most efficient and effective learning experience possible.

A0 GENERAL TERMS

Action

Any specific task or step taken to progress towards achieving a goal.

In the ICOR® methodology, the "world of action" refers to the domain where deliberate and strategic activities are executed and completed to achieve desired outcomes. It encompasses the practical implementation of plans, where tasks are performed, progress is tracked, and results are generated.

This "world" is characterized by a focus on doing, where intentions and strategies are translated into tangible, measurable actions that drive productivity and success.

Core Apps

Essential software tools that offer a wide range of features and serve as the primary repository for your information and action, acting as your Single Source of Truth. They hold crucial data and functionalities, making them irreplaceable without a suitable replacement.

Switching Core Apps is often painful, expensive, and risky, so it's usually better to stick with your current Core App despite any issues.

ICOR®

ICOR® (Input, Control, Output, Refine) is a comprehensive, holistic methodology designed to help busy professionals maximize efficiency and productivity.

ICOR® aims to empower busy professionals to develop and maintain a seamless, tailored productivity system, optimizing performance, minimizing burnout, and with any tools.

While it focuses on improving business and enterprise operations, it also positively impacts personal lives.

ICOR® Framework

The ICOR® Framework is a structured approach for creating an optimized productivity system tailored to individual needs.

It divides the world of productivity into four key areas (Personal, Business, Information, and Action) covering all possible combinations:

- **PKM (Personal Knowledge Management)** is for storing personal information; anything unique to you and initially not impacting anyone else.
- **BKM (Business Knowledge Management)** is for team-related information. Anything you need to share with your co-workers.
- **PPM (Personal Project Management)** is for managing your own tasks, the ones that only affect you.
- **BPM (Business Project Management)** is for managing tasks that affect both you and your team.

The framework helps busy professionals visualize and organize their tools within these areas, identifying overlaps and gaps, ensuring each tool serves a specific purpose without redundancy.

The ICOR® Framework promotes efficiency and effectiveness, aiming to streamline tool usage for maximum productivity.

ICOR® Journey

The ICOR® Journey is a straightforward, step-by-step guide to implementing the ICOR® methodology with ease.

Available through the Paperless Movement® Membership, this journey is broken down into a set of comprehensive and sequential courses that aim to empower busy professionals to develop and maintain a seamless, tailored productivity system, optimizing performance and minimizing burnout.

ICOR® Note-taking Framework

The ICOR® Note-taking Framework is a streamlined note-taking tool designed for busy professionals.

It simplifies the note-taking process into six easy-to-follow workflows tailored to common daily scenarios, making it more practical and actionable than traditional methods.

The ICOR® Note-taking Framework is visualized as a circle divided into these six areas, each with three levels (good, better, best) to assess the effectiveness of note-taking tools.

Busy professionals use the ICOR® Note-taking Framework to map their current tools, aiming to achieve the "best" level in each workflow and streamline their tool stack for maximum efficiency and goal achievement.

ICOR® Stage 1: Input

Input is the first stage in the ICOR® methodology, where the focus is on capturing and integrating information from two primary sources, the Outer World and the Inner World, into your productivity system.

ICOR® Stage 2: Control

Control is the second stage in the ICOR® methodology.

It focuses on turning the information you've gathered into useful knowledge.

By mastering the Control stage, you establish a reliable and effective system that not only manages information but also drives consistent and purposeful action towards your goals.

ICOR® Stage 3: Output
Output is the third stage in the ICOR® methodology.

This is where you transition from collecting and processing information to taking concrete actions, with a focus on efficiently planning, managing, and carrying out these actions to achieve your goals.

ICOR® Stage 4: Refine
Refine is the fourth and final stage of the ICOR® methodology, focusing on continuously improving your productivity system.

Refining is an ongoing process, crucial for transforming and elevating your productivity system beyond its initial setup. It combines the best aspects of information management and actionable workflows, ensuring your system unleashes its full potential and evolves with your needs.

Information
Essential data, insights, and reflections can be gathered from the external environment (Outer World) or from one's own thoughts (Inner World).

ICOR® envisions an integrated and structured information ecosystem where data is meticulously managed and converted into practical actions. When processed effectively, this raw material transforms into actionable steps towards achieving specific goals.

The information ecosystem in ICOR® is dynamic, continuously refined through iterative processes to maintain peak performance and minimize energy waste, supporting both professional and personal growth.

Intermediate Tool

An Intermediate Tool is a temporary yet efficient tool used to capture, process, or manage information and actions when your primary tool, the Single Source of Truth (SSOT), is less accessible or effective for the task at hand.

It can be used at any time when the intermediate tool offers a more streamlined experience for handling information or executing actions.

Later, the information or actions can be transferred or organized into the SSOT, ensuring a smooth workflow with minimal friction while maintaining productivity and organization.

Productivity System End to End

A productivity system end to end is the one designed to help individuals or teams efficiently manage their information, action, and communication from start to finish.

It integrates multiple concepts, workflows, techniques, and tools to streamline business processes, optimize time management, and ensure that goals are always met.

Satellite Apps

Software tools that enhance Core Apps by reducing friction or addressing specific weaknesses for tasks such as capturing, automating workflows, or linking different systems. Unlike Core Apps, Satellite Apps can be easily swapped when a better option is found, as they have minimal impact on the overall productivity system.

Single Source of Truth (SSOT)

A Single Source of Truth (SSOT) is a definitive reference point for storing and retrieving information or action, ensuring clarity and simplicity by organizing a productivity system in a way that avoids confusion and enhances productivity.

The 3-Layer Approach

At the Paperless Movement®, we use a 3-layer approach to help busy professionals understand and implement our ICOR® methodology effectively.

This structured approach makes it easier and faster to grasp and apply ICOR®.

Our three layers (Concepts, Workflows, and Implementation) guide you from understanding the basics to applying practical solutions:

- **Concepts**. We begin with the fundamental principles that form the backbone of an effective ICOR® productivity system.
- **Workflows**. Next, we turn these principles into actionable processes that you can follow.
- **Implementation**. Finally, we provide practical guidance on using specific tools and techniques to apply these workflows.

This approach saves you time and provides tangible solutions that become more valuable as you integrate them into your daily life.

Utility Apps

Non-essential tools that boost your productivity without being crucial to how your productivity system works, so it stays intact even if you stop using them. Examples include browsers like Arc or launchers like Raycast.

A1 INPUT

Note

A written record that captures important information, decisions, insights, or action items from various business-related activities.

Notes can be text, images, audio, videos, sketches, or digital formats.

Note-taking

The art of capturing information from various sources in a manner that prepares you for remembering, comprehending, and most critically, taking action.

A2 CONTROL

BKM (Business Knowledge Management)

Business Knowledge Management (BKM) is a strategic approach that involves systematically collecting, organizing, sharing, and using knowledge within a company to boost productivity, efficiency, and innovation.

Essentially, BKM aims to unify and streamline information and action, making sure that the right knowledge is available to the right people at the right time and in the right context.

The key strength of BKM is its ability to enhance the collective intelligence of an organization and improve team communication.

BKM helps teams work together seamlessly, reduces unnecessary work, eliminates inefficiencies, and fosters a culture of continuous improvement and learning.

This comprehensive approach not only aids in decision-making and problem-solving but also drives growth and provides a competitive edge, ultimately leading to a state of peak productivity.

In the ICOR® Framework, the BKM area is where you place the tools you use to share information with your team.

Bucket

A Bucket is a storage space for various ideas and information on different topics or projects that don't need immediate action. It helps organize these ideas for easier retrieval and understanding later.

Unlike an Inbox, which requires prompt attention and regular processing, a Bucket is meant to support action when needed, not to prompt it.

Context

Context is the background and circumstances of a piece of information that help in storing, retrieving, and using it effectively.

It involves:

1. **Tracing**. Identifying the source (e.g., tweet, meeting, article) and capturing details about it.
2. **Integrating**. Connecting new information to your existing knowledge in a meaningful way.

This approach ensures information is easily accessible and useful, enhancing productivity and clarity.

Deep Thinking

The thorough exploration and understanding of concepts, involving detailed analysis, synthesis of ideas, and visualization to gain meaningful insights and solutions.

Inbox

An Inbox is a temporary holding place for any type of item (information or action) when you cannot immediately store it in its designated final location, its Single Source of Truth (SSOT).

It serves as an essential component of any productivity system, allowing you to capture and organize items without disrupting your workflow.

Effective use of an Inbox involves regularly processing and relocating its contents to their proper places (SSOT), ensuring your productivity system remains organized and efficient.

Inner World

The Inner World refers to information that originates directly from you, such as your own thoughts, ideas, or notes taken during meetings. You are the creator of this content.

Key Element

An essential aspect of your life or work that requires focused attention.

Key Elements include critical areas such as your company, business partners, or personal health.

Information impacting these Key Elements should be prioritized to ensure it supports your overall well-being and professional growth.

Outer World

The Outer World refers to information you encounter through external sources like internet articles, books, podcasts, or YouTube videos.

This is content created by others, but you can add your own thoughts and annotations to it.

PKM (Personal Knowledge Management)

A systematic approach to discovering, capturing, processing, and organizing information to enhance understanding and facilitate actionable steps toward achieving personal and professional goals.

In the ICOR® Framework, the PKM area is where you keep personal tools for storing information unique to you and not affecting anyone else.

Shallow Thinking

The quick capture and retrieval of information, processed almost instantaneously, often using simple methods like tagging or categorization to manage the fast pace of daily work.

The Capturing Beast

The Capturing Beast is a mental model designed to help busy professionals filter and prioritize information. It uses three key layers to determine what deserves your attention:

1. **Current Projects**. Focus on information directly relevant to your ongoing projects.
2. **Key Elements**. Prioritize information that impacts crucial aspects of your life, like your company or health.
3. **Topics**. Concentrate on a limited number of subjects you want to explore deeply.

This approach helps manage information overload, reduces FOMO (Fear of Missing Out), and ensures focus on what truly matters.

The Knowledge Management Cycle

The Knowledge Management Cycle is a structured workflow designed to manage and use personal knowledge effectively. It involves five sequential stages:

1. **Discover**. Identify and find valuable information relevant to your goals.
2. **Capture**. Record and save this information systematically.
3. **Process**. Organize and analyze the captured information to derive meaningful insights.
4. **Act**. Take concrete steps based on the processed information to achieve your goals.
5. **Share**. Communicate and distribute the knowledge to benefit others and reinforce your own understanding.

This cycle ensures that information is not only stored

but actively used to drive personal productivity and goal achievement.

The Thought Lab

A mental model within your Personal Knowledge Management (PKM) system used during the Process stage to evaluate and filter captured information.

It involves reflecting on whether the information is valuable or just clutter by asking key questions about its significance and relevance to your Key Elements, Current Projects, or Topics.

If the information is deemed valuable, it moves to the next stage for action; if not, it is either discarded or stored with context for potential future use.

This approach ensures that only useful information is kept, enhancing the effectiveness of your PKM system.

Topic

A subject of interest you choose to explore further, related to your business or personal life.

In the context of The Capturing Beast mental model, you can easily think of dozens, hundreds, or even thousands of Topics, but this can be overwhelming and counterproductive.

That's why we recommend limiting your focus to just three Topics at a time, allowing focused attention and significant progress. You can review and adjust these Topics whenever you like, for example, monthly, quarterly, or even yearly. It's up to you.

Examples of Topics include, for example, productivity, marketing, or CRM tools.

Regularly review and adjust your chosen Topics to ensure they remain relevant and impactful for your goals.

A3 OUTPUT

Balance

Balance is managing daily and weekly planning to prevent anxiety, stress, and burnout, allowing optimal performance.

Handle 7-10 tasks a day, with 4-6 hours for planned work and 2-4 hours as buffer time for unexpected events.

Align tasks with goals, adjust expectations to reality, and distribute tasks evenly throughout your day and week to match your energy levels and circumstances.

Batching

The practice of grouping similar tasks together and performing them consecutively to maximize efficiency, reduce transition time, and minimize distractions.

This approach leverages the brain's ability to focus on one type of activity at a time, thereby enhancing overall productivity.

BPM (Business Project Management)

Business Project Management is the structured approach to planning, executing, and managing projects within a business environment.

It involves setting clear goals, prioritizing tasks, and systematically converting ideas into actionable items.

By applying ICOR®, BPM ensures effective communication, minimizes disruptions, and enables teams to work efficiently and asynchronously, focusing on achieving swift and stress-free outcomes.

In the ICOR® Framework, the BPM area is where you place the tools you use to manage your Projects, Workstreams, and Operations.

Calendar

A calendar is a tool used to organize and track time-sensitive commitments such as events, meetings, and appointments.

It helps record constraints and mandatory activities, ensuring that these fixed commitments are managed effectively.

Examples of calendar tools include Google Calendar, iCal, or Outlook.

Daily Planning

Daily Planning is the process of focusing on the tasks planned for the current day, ensuring a structured and productive execution of these tasks.

It involves reviewing the tasks listed in your Weekly Planning, assessing their feasibility, identifying the most critical task of the day (Highlight of the Day), ordering tasks sequentially to avoid multitasking, and committing to their execution.

This approach encourages focusing on today's tasks without being distracted by past or future concerns.

Daily Routine

A daily Routine is a structured sequence of tasks you perform regularly at specific times each day.

It serves as a foundation for your productivity system, helping you transition from reacting to events to proactively managing your day.

By following these prearranged tasks on autopilot, you save mental energy and ensure nothing is overlooked.

Daily routines typically include morning, afternoon, and end-of-day tasks such as planning, checking inboxes, delegating tasks, and reflecting on your day.

They provide a sense of control and consistency, crucial for maintaining productivity and achieving long-term goals.

Deep Work
Deep Work involves focusing intensely on cognitively demanding tasks without distractions.

It maximizes productivity, improves skills, generates new value, and is difficult to replicate.

Examples include strategic planning, product design, writing detailed reports, or learning new skills.

Goal
A Goal is a non-actionable Output Element that represents a stable direction or target to achieve.

It organizes all the Output Elements in the hierarchy to align with the overall direction, providing a clear path to follow in your Project Management system.

Highlight of the Day
The Highlight of the Day is a specific task, selected from your Weekly Goals, that you choose to complete each day, ensuring consistent progress towards your goals.

Operations
Operations are a non-actionable Output Element that covers tasks outside the scope of Projects and Workstreams, such as, for example, administrative duties or unique asset creation.

It groups related tasks to ensure the business keeps running. Example: administrative tasks.

Output Elements
Output Elements are objects designed to streamline the organization and management of tasks within a Project Management system.

They are split into two main categories:

1. **Actionable elements**. These require execution and to be completed to produce deliverables.
2. **Non-actionable elements**. These act as containers to provide clarity and help switch between broad overviews and detailed analyses.

Here's how Output Elements break down:

- Goals (non-actionable).
- Projects (non-actionable).
- Workstreams (non-actionable).
- Operations (non-actionable).
- Tasks (actionable).

Output Formula

The Output Formula is a mental model within ICOR® that enables the creation and organization of Output Elements through two main approaches: Bottom-Up and Top-Down.

In the Bottom-Up approach, you begin with specific tasks and progressively group them into higher-level Output Elements like Projects, Workstreams, Operations, and ultimately Goals.

In the Top-Down approach, you start with a broad Goal and break it down into significant actions, further refining them into manageable tasks.

This flexibility allows for efficient Project Management and adapts to the varying needs and complexities that busy professionals face daily.

PEA (Plan, Execute, Align)

PEA is a mental model designed to streamline priority setting in Project Management by focusing on Time Management. It's a key component of a larger mental model called The Execution Beast.

Instead of using traditional labels like high, medium, or low priority, PEA helps you answer three key questions:

1. **Plan**. "WHEN am I going to do this?"
2. **Execute**. "WHAT do I do now?"
3. **Align**. "Am I doing what I SHOULD be doing?"

This approach ensures you prioritize tasks effectively, avoiding confusion and ensuring all tasks, regardless of perceived priority, contribute to overall success.

Planner

A planner is a tool designed for managing your time and organizing multiple activities, including tasks.

It supports Time Management techniques like Time Blocking, allowing you to schedule and prioritize tasks around your fixed commitments.

Planners often integrate with calendar views to help manage both tasks and events seamlessly.

Examples of planner tools include Akiflow or Sunsama.

PPM (Personal Project Management or Task Management)

The organization, tracking, and completion of work-related tasks that are solely your professional responsibility.

Importantly, this does not include tasks related to your personal life.

It focuses on boosting your productivity and effectiveness in achieving business goals through efficient daily and weekly organization.

In the ICOR® Framework, the PPM area is where you place the tools you use to manage these tasks.

Project

A Project is a non-actionable Output Element encapsulating

one-time tasks with a clear start and end date, leading to a specific outcome.

It groups related tasks to ensure they align with one or more Goals.

Example: Designing a product, which concludes with the final design.

Reminder
An alarm set to alert you when a Task or Speedy needs to be executed on a specific date and time.

Reminders jog your memory and can be used for other items, such as events.

Sequentiality
The practice of focusing on one task at a time, completing it before moving on to the next.

This approach aligns with our natural cognitive tendencies, reducing stress, mistakes, and improving productivity.

It encourages focus, accomplishment, and effective prioritization, making it a fundamental principle in effective Task Management systems.

Shallow Work
Shallow Work refers to tasks that require minimal brainpower and are often performed while distracted or with low energy.

They are routine, easily replicable, and don't create much new value although you cannot avoid them.

Examples include responding to emails, routine administrative duties, attending meetings, or browsing the web.

Speedy
A Task that can be completed in less than 15 minutes. Speedies require minimal planning and are considered Shallow Work.

Task

A Task is an actionable Output Element requiring execution to produce deliverables.

It is a specific action that needs to be completed, ranging from a quick 15-minute action to something that takes up to three hours.

It's highly recommended to start task names with an action verb. This makes it clear what needs to be done, defines the outcome, and helps you quickly identify tasks in your productivity system.

For example, instead of just "Report A," use "Write Report A."

Tasks under 15 minutes are called Speedies.

Task Management

The process of organizing, tracking, and completing personal work tasks to improve productivity and achieve business goals, focusing solely on professional responsibilities and not personal life tasks.

The Execution Beast

The Execution Beast is an ICOR® mental model designed to guarantee you and your team complete all the tasks needed to achieve your goals.

It operates through two key steps:

1. **Creating Initial Output Elements**. At the start of each quarter, define clear Goals and outline Projects, Workstreams, or Operations to achieve them. Set specific tasks, start, and end dates for each element.
2. **Using PEA (Plan, Execute, Align)**.
   Plan. Schedule tasks weekly and assign specific days to ensure a realistic plan.
   Execute. Focus on executing tasks daily, considering energy levels, urgency, quick tasks (Speedies), and unexpected events.
   Align. Continuously ensure tasks align with overall goals through regular reviews.

This system promotes continuous progress and peak performance by emphasizing quarterly planning, weekly goal-setting (Weekly Goals), and daily execution.

The Idea Incubator

The Idea Incubator is a streamlined mental model within a Project Management system designed to transform ideas into actionable results through four key steps: Capture, Evaluate, Plan, and Execute.

It emphasizes the importance of not ignoring any idea, no matter how small, and provides a structured process to ensure each idea is captured in a Single Source of Truth, evaluated for its potential, planned for implementation, and executed efficiently.

This system enhances team collaboration and productivity by integrating ideas seamlessly into existing workflows, ensuring valuable ideas are not lost and can be quickly acted upon to achieve goals with minimal effort.

The Team Communication System
The Team Communication system is designed to coordinate team efforts through asynchronous Project Management.

This system allows team members to work independently while staying informed about overall progress and team actions.

It relies on a Single Source of Truth; a central, transparent repository of accurate information accessible to everyone on the team.

Key practices include minimizing interruptions, implementing task reviews, centralizing Output Elements, respecting conversation threads, and using custom views to align team Goals and progress.

This system enhances collaboration, efficiency, and overall team performance by providing clear workflows and the right tools.

Time Blocking

Time Blocking is a Time Management technique where you divide your day into dedicated blocks of time, each reserved for specific tasks or groups of tasks (Routines, for example).

This method helps you focus exclusively on one slot at a time, building a system that is both structured and flexible.

The main goal is to provide a clear focus at any moment, helping you prioritize effectively and achieve your Weekly Goals.

Time Management

Time Management refers to the strategic process of planning and exercising conscious control over the amount of time spent on specific activities to increase effectiveness, efficiency, and productivity.

It involves prioritizing tasks, setting goals, delegating responsibilities, scheduling, and organizing resources to optimize one's workday and achieve a balance between work demands and personal life.

Effective Time Management helps busy professionals manage their workload, reduce stress, meet deadlines, and enhance overall performance.

Subtask

A Subtask is a smaller, actionable item derived from a larger, complex Task.

It starts with an action verb and is used to break down the main Task into manageable parts, making the overall Task easier to complete and organize.

The main Task is renamed without a verb and often written in all caps to signify it contains Subtasks.

Weekly Goals

The tasks you plan to finish or, at least, dedicate as much time as possible, within the week.

Weekly Goals should be linked to the Goals in your productivity system, ensuring alignment between your daily tasks and overall objectives.

Weekly Planning

Weekly Planning is a structured approach to organizing your week, ensuring you know exactly what tasks to do and when to do them.

It involves five sequential steps:

1. **Brain Zen**. Achieve peace of mind by thoroughly reviewing and listing all tasks from your Project and Task Management systems.
2. **Goal Alignment**. Identify and prioritize five crucial tasks (Weekly Goals) that align with your overall objectives.
3. **Schedule**. Assign each task to a specific day, focusing on when to do each task.
4. **Balance**. Ensure each day's plan includes 4-6 hours of planned work (Weekly Goals and Routines) and 2-4 hours of buffer time.
5. **Re-balance**. Perform a final check to ensure your plan is realistic and achievable.

By following these steps, you create a clear, manageable, and effective plan for your week.

Weekly Review

A Weekly Review is a brief, efficient check-in where you execute your Weekly Planning by ensuring all tasks are up to date with planned execution dates.

This review takes just a few minutes if your Task Management system is set up correctly.

It helps maintain organization and productivity without the need for lengthy or formal reviews, as the system stays current through regular interaction.

Workstream

In the context of Output, ICOR®'s third stage, a Workstream is a non-actionable Output Element consisting of ongoing, repetitive tasks executed sequentially.

It groups related tasks to ensure they align with one or more Goals.

Example: Content creation, such as producing YouTube videos, where each cycle follows the exact same steps.

A4 REFINE

Automation

Automation is the process of streamlining and simplifying processes to make them more efficient and intuitive.

It involves using various tools and techniques to handle repetitive and complex tasks automatically, freeing up time and energy for more important activities.

The goal of Automation is to create workflows that are logical, sustainable, and reflect the way our minds work, ultimately enhancing productivity and efficiency.

Momentum

Momentum is a state of productivity characterized by intense focus, mental clarity, and heightened motivation, leading to efficient and high-quality task completion.

It emerges spontaneously and cannot be scheduled, but when it occurs, it enables faster task completion and superior results by immersing you in the present moment.

Optimization

Optimization is the process of improving a task, system, or process by enhancing its efficiency, focusing on achieving the best possible performance or outcome, distinct from simplification, which aims to make things easier rather than more efficient.

Procedure

A specific set of instructions for executing a Process, Workflow, or Workstream, ensuring tasks are performed consistently and efficiently.

(Business) Process
An organized task performed by people or machines to achieve a specific business goal, ranging from simple to complex.

SOP (Standard Operating Procedure)
A collection of related procedures providing comprehensive guidelines for complex tasks, ensuring consistency and standardization.

Workflow
A collection of processes that gives a broader perspective on complex tasks, outlining inputs and outputs.

Workstream
A Workstream is a way to organize and manage multiple related workflows more effectively.

It acts as a container that groups together these workflows, especially when they become complex, making it easier to coordinate and oversee everything.

ABOUT THE AUTHOR

Tom Solid & Paco Cantero

TOM SOLID
Dr. Thomas Roedl, also known as Tom Solid, is a recognized expert in corporate efficiency and productivity. With years of experience as a Business Analyst, Tom has a proven track record of significantly improving cross-department performance (up to 60%). Since founding the Paperless Movement® in 2018, he has helped thousands of clients take their productivity to the next level through his coaching and expertise.

PACO CANTERO
Paco Cantero, a Computer Science Engineer, began his coding journey at eight years old and has deep expertise in technology and process optimization. With experience at PriceWaterhouse Coopers and Accenture, Paco now manages four businesses and a team of over 70 people, showing the impact of the ICOR® methodology. In 2022, he became a co-founder of the Paperless Movement®, where he continues to share his insights in the productivity space.

Printed in Great Britain
by Amazon